I LOVE

—A—

SUNBURNT COUNTRY

THE DIARIES OF
DOROTHEA MACKELLAR

Publishing History of the Works of Dorothea Mackellar

POETRY

The Closed Door
Australasian Authors' Agency, Melbourne, 1911

Witch-maid
J. M. Dent & Sons Ltd, London, 1914

Dream Harbour
Longmans, Green and Co, London, 1923

Fancy Dress
Angus & Robertson Ltd, Sydney, 1926

NOVELS

Outlaw's Luck
Mills & Boon Ltd, London, 1913

The Little Blue Devil
in collaboration with Ruth Bedford,
Alston Rivers Ltd, London, 1912

Two's Company
in collaboration with Ruth Bedford,
Alston Rivers Ltd, London, 1914

I LOVE
A
SUNBURNT
COUNTRY

THE DIARIES OF
DOROTHEA MACKELLAR

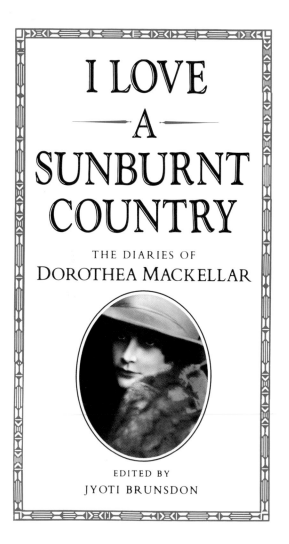

EDITED BY
JYOTI BRUNSDON

ANGUS
& ROBERTSON
PUBLISHERS

ANGUS & ROBERTSON PUBLISHERS

Unit 4, Eden Park, 31 Waterloo Road,
North Ryde, NSW, Australia 2113; and
16 Golden Square, London W1R 4BN,
United Kingdom

First published in Australia
by Angus & Robertson Publishers in 1990

Copyright © Diaries Mrs B.K. Strang, Mr C. Dredge 1990
Copyright © Introduction and editing Jyoti Brunsdon 1990

National Library of Australia
Cataloguing-in-publication data.

Mackellar, Dorothea, 1885-1968.
    I love a sunburnt country : the diaries of Dorothea Mackellar.

    ISBN 0 207 16170 4.

    1. Mackellar, Dorothea, 1885-1968—Diaries.
    2. Poets, Australian—20th century—
    Diaries. I. Brunsdon, Jyoti, 1941- .
    II. Title.

A 821'.2

Typeset in 10/14 Garamond
Printed in Hong Kong

Contents

To Kath, who thought it was
a good idea

My Country

The love of field and coppice
Of green and shaded lanes
Of ordered woods and gardens
Is running in your veins —
Strong love of grey-blue distance
Brown streams and soft dim skies . . .
I know but cannot share it,
My love is otherwise.

I love a sunburnt country
A land of sweeping plains
Of ragged mountain-ranges
Of droughts and flooding rains.
I love her far horizons
I love her jewel-sea,
Her beauty and her terror —
The wide brown land for me!*

The stark white ringbarked forests
All tragic 'neath the moon,
The sapphire-misted mountains
The hot gold hush of noon —
Green tangle of the brushes
Where lithe lianas coil
And orchid-laden tree-ferns
Smother the crimson soil.

Core of my heart, my country —
Her pitiless blue sky,
When sick at heart, around us
We see the cattle die . . .
And then the grey clouds gather
And we can bless again,
The drumming of an army,
The steady, soaking rain.

Core of my heart, my Country,
Young land of Rainbow Gold —
For flood and fire and famine
She pays us back three-fold . . .
Over the thirsty paddocks
Watch, after many days
A filmy veil of greenness
That thickens as you gaze . . .

An opal-hearted country,
A wilful, lavish land —
Ah, you who have not loved her
You cannot understand . . .
. . . The world is fair and splendid
But wheresoe'er I die
I know to what brown country
My homing thoughts will fly!

me!: In the manuscript, this line first read: "The dear brown land for me". She changed "dear" to "wide", writing one word over the other. "My Country" was originally entitled "Core of My Heart".

OPPOSITE: *A Summer's Day* Hans Heysen

Introduction

By the time of her death in 1968, at the age of 82, Dorothea Mackellar's name had become part of Australia's history. Her fame rested on a single poem written in her youth: "My Country". Originally entitled "Core of My Heart", the poem was first published in the English journal the *Spectator* in September 1908. Within weeks it had been reprinted in the Australian nationalist publication *Call*, for its verses reflected the ardent spirit of nationalism which had awakened with Federation in 1901. They presented images of Australia that resonated perfectly with popular sentiment: "I love a sunburnt country/a land of sweeping plains/. . . Core of my heart, my country . . ."

During the years of the First World War "My Country" became widely known in Australia. Soon it became, too, the means by which Australians abroad could express their nostalgia for home. On November 10 1923 the *Sydney Morning Herald* reported:

> Sitting at a dinner table in New York, it was the privilege of the writer of this article to see eighty Australians, with Senator Pearce leading them, rise to their feet and cheer the recitation of Miss Dorothea's best-known patriotic poem . . .

By the 1930s "My Country" had become an integral part of Australian education. With changes to the education system in the early 1960s, it began to disappear from school syllabuses, but by this time the phrases "a sunburnt country" and "the wide brown land" had become deeply rooted in the Australian psyche. At one time it was even suggested that "My Country" deserved the ultimate accolade, that of becoming Australia's national anthem. Yet of the author little was known, as I discovered when I endeavoured to research her life.

Early in 1987 I was asked to provide a libretto for an opera by Alan Holley based on the life of Dorothea Mackellar and commissioned by the New South Wales council of Warringah Shire as part of its Bicentennial celebrations. I cheerfully agreed to the project, imagining that it would be a simple matter to find a biography of Dorothea Mackellar. No such work existed. In lieu of a biography, I bought a copy of a selection of her poems, *My Country and Other Poems of Dorothea Mackellar*. It contained a brief and intriguing

OPPOSITE: *Dorothea, c.1910*

introduction by Adrienne Matzenik, Dorothea Mackellar's nurse during the last years of her life, which described Dorothea Mackellar's wealthy background, travels and romances. Perhaps the story of Dorothea's love for the English banker and poet Patrick Chalmers might be the basis for an opera? But the details were scanty, and I resorted to the well-worn device of requesting information through the columns of the *Sydney Morning Herald.*

Of those who initially contacted me, few could substantially help in what I now thought of as my search for Dorothea. Then in quick succession I was put in touch with Mrs Dorothea Hedger, one of Dorothea Mackellar's god-children, and was contacted by Mrs Kath Strang, a cousin and current co-holder of copyright in the works of Dorothea Mackellar. Mrs Hedger and Mrs Strang were from the outset unstintingly generous in their assistance, though both belonged to a generation younger than Dorothea and could not verify events of more than 70 years ago.

Mrs Hedger described her childhood holidays with her godmother at Lovett Bay on Sydney's Pittwater, of playing on the rocky shores, of long quiet hours spent fishing from a rowing boat or exploring the bushland hill behind Tarrangaua, the house Dorothea frequently withdrew to in middle age. Beautiful, but not the stuff of opera. I yearned for just one little axe murder. Mrs Strang lent me papers spanning a century of Mackellar history and patiently answered my questions. She told me she had lodged manuscripts, correspondence and Mackellar memorabilia, including one diary, with the Mitchell Library.

As I waited for a reader's ticket to the Library's special collections, I read Dorothea Mackellar's poems, published in four little volumes between 1911 and 1926, and reflected on the fact that, whilst almost everyone I spoke to was familiar with "My Country", scarcely anyone could quote another poem by Dorothea Mackellar. In fact, apart from the works of A. B. Paterson, very few could quote any Australian poetry written before 1908. Beyond the sphere of academia, "My Country" had, with few exceptions, eclipsed more than a century of Australian poetry.

On its publication Dorothea Mackellar was hailed as

> the first real Australian patriot . . . the first genuine Australian songster . . . This [is] not merely because her subjects are Australian but because she sings as if

she were singing of her own to her own, and because all real Australians throughout the whole of Australia will hear an echo in their own hearts when they hear her sing. Besides this, she has, more than anyone who has yet written in Australia, the real poetic gift of insight and expression . . . a rarer and diviner touch, a loftier and more dignified personality than any of our previous singers.*

The premiere of the opera was set for October 1988, and Alan Holley was anxious for a libretto. I prepared an incomplete text based on the romance between Patrick and Dorothea, as described by Adrienne Matzenik, promising more details soon. Eventually the day arrived when a closed box was before me in the Library. According to the contents list, the box contained diaries, a notebook, a commonplace book (her scrapbook) and a letter book. It was an unforgettable moment to find not the single diary Mrs Strang recalled, but ten. I took out the smallest—for 1955. Most of the pages were blank. Here and there was a note of a dental appointment, a lunch or a visit. I took out another—a little book just 6 x 4 centimetres—and opened it. Nearly every line of every page was filled with minuscule writing. The year was 1910. I took another diary and another. Every day described. Some of the ink was faded, much of the writing not easily legible, yet clearly here was a full record of many years of Dorothea Mackellar's life.

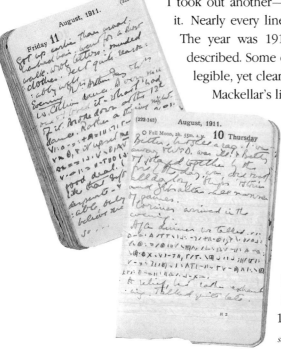

What had she written about Patrick Chalmers? I opened the diary for 1913 and was delighted to find references to "Pat". But dipping into the diaries at random made little sense, and it did not take long to realise I would have to start from the beginning.

In the weeks leading up to this particular day Mrs Strang had suggested that I might publish my research. In the diaries, surely, was a book about Dorothea Mackellar better than any I could hope to write. They covered most of the period between 1910 and 1920, and also 1927 to 1930 and 1955. (I

singers: Commonweal, November 1 1911.

ABOVE: *Pages from Dorothea's diaries*

later found one for 1941 stored elsewhere in the Mitchell Library.) I discussed with Mrs Strang the idea of editing the diaries for 1910 to 1918 and was given her blessing.

If my first unforgettable moment was the discovery of the diaries, the second came when I turned a page to find much of the entry for the next day in code. Hieroglyphics? It certainly was no language I recognised. In the days that followed, I copied many coded entries, with a vague optimism that their meaning might become clear as time went by. Then came the day when I read the entry: "Dined with ⊠." Because of the context, I thought the symbol ⊠ might be a P. The time had come to try a little code-cracking.

The entry I took looked like this:

$$⊠ \, / \, / \, T : / \, O \, \_\, | : ⊞ \, + T = \backslash \, | : V — = :$$
$$\rceil \, | \, | \, ⊞ : = / : + ⊞ \, V \div ⊠ \, ⊠ \, X :$$

It seemed that : could indicate word endings.

I tried fitting Ps into the final word:

$$+ ⊞ \, V — P \, P \, X$$

If the P was correct, then the only letter to sit comfortably at the end of the word would be a Y:

$$+ ⊞ \, V — P \, P \, Y$$

Was this word "UNHAPPY"? I already suspected that / and | were vowels, perhaps E and O. I tried, but it didn't look like anything! This was like solving a crossword puzzle. I tried again, and suddenly I saw it:

POOR OLD NURSIE HAS
BEEN SO UNHAPPY

It fitted the text. And now I had fourteen letters of the alphabet. I fitted these into other sections in code and soon the puzzle was solved. I did not know that luck had been on my side. Only much later did I realise that ⊠ stood not for "Patrick" but for "Philip".

The work of transcription began in earnest. From the very first entry, it was apparent that one side of Dorothea's life was privilege. It did not take long to realise that the other was tremendous restriction. I was introduced to a world where a woman of 28 still required a chaperone, to an era of muff-mending and tidying the jewel cabinet, where gardens were sat in, not worked in, Dad had dinner with Lord Kitchener, and on a clear day the British Empire went on forever. And a world where so many things could not be spoken of. Her diaries were a repository for thoughts which craved expression and yet could not be shared. To keep her secrets safe from prying eyes, maybe in part to keep them safe even from herself, anything that might have been considered indelicate or indiscreet was usually written in code—and then with considerable restraint. (In this edition of Dorothea's diaries, bold type has been used for the deciphered code.*)

Assisted by my friend Jenya Osborne, I started with the tiny diaries of 1910 and 1911, and Dorothea's youthful optimism spurred us on when we were tired or frustrated by our inability to decipher the brusque and often hurriedly written entries. In 1912, in anticipation of a long sea voyage to England, Dorothea acquired a large notebook. No longer limited to a single page for each day's events, her writing took on the character of a journal. Whether in Australia or England, a rhythm emerged to her life as she moved regularly between the sophistication of the city and the simplicity of the country. It became clear that boredom and emotional suppression affected her health. We soon learnt, however, that Dorothea had a lively sense of humour, and at times Jenya and

DOROTHEA'S CODE

A	—	H	∨	O	/	V	⬯
B	⌐	I	\	P	⊠	W	△
C	⌐	J	□	Q	⊥	X	▽
D	⌐	K	◇	R	⊤	Y	✕
E	|	L	○	S	=	Z	∞
F	⌐	M	⊕	T	‖	!	☆
G	∧	N	⊞	U	+	.	×

OPPOSITE: *Dorothea, about sixteen*

I were gripped by a hilarity which seemed close to a sin in the quiet gravity of the Mitchell Library.

If breaking the code was like solving a crossword puzzle, the diaries themselves were an enormous jigsaw—and I had no idea what the final picture might reveal. Who were the people about whom she wrote? Where were the houses? What did it all mean? Some things came clear as Jenya and I continued to transcribe, other small mysteries were solved by reading correspondence and other papers in the collection. Some of the *dramatis personae* were identified through contemporary newspapers and *Who's Who*, some from the *Australian Dictionary of Biography*. I met Mrs Helen Rutledge and Mr Reg Broun, both of whom had known Dorothea, and they kindly placed their prodigious memories at my service. But some mysteries still remain.

The diaries dated from 1910, when Dorothea was 24, but a single page from 1909, caught between two pages of the 1910 book, indicated that earlier diaries had existed. Maybe, like large sections of the diaries for 1914 to 1916, they had disintegrated with time. As I traced her life towards its beginning, I realised that in order to see Dorothea Mackellar with any clarity, I needed to know more of the family into which she was born.

Dorothea's grandfather was Frederick Mackellar, a doctor who had left Scotland in 1838 to try his luck in the colonies, and who had prospered in private practice in Pitt Street, Sydney. In 1844 he married Isobel, wealthy widow of William McGarvie, one of the founders of the *Sydney Morning Herald*, and on December 5 of that year, their son Charles Kinnaird, Dorothea's father, was born. Over the next few years Frederick Mackellar began to involve himself in a number of successful commercial and pastoral ventures.

Charles Mackellar was educated at Sydney Grammar School, following which he spent several years on a family property at Port Macquarie. In his early twenties he sailed for Scotland and studies at the University of Glasgow, graduating with degrees in medicine and surgery in 1871. He returned to Sydney, and in 1873 accepted his first appointment at the hospital then known as the Sydney Infirmary and Dispensary and later renamed Sydney Hospital.

By 1884 Charles Mackellar was a director of Sydney Hospital, a position he held until 1903, and in 1886 he became a director of the Royal Prince Alfred Hospital. Between 1881 and 1885 he also held numerous significant positions, including chairman of the Immigration Board, a member of the Board of Pharmacy and the Medical Board, official visitor to Sydney's two hospitals for the insane, and president of the Board of Health. In August 1885 he resigned from these appointments and was nominated to the Legislative Council, a position he held until the last year of his life, apart from a brief period in late 1903 when he filled the vacancy created in the Commonwealth Senate by the appointment of R. E. O'Connor as the first judge of the Supreme Court of Australia.

Both in public and private life, Dr Charles Mackellar was dedicated to the welfare of under-privileged and mentally handicapped children. Like his father, however, he had keen business instincts and he also held many commercial positions, including president of the Bank of New South Wales, and director of a number of insurance companies and of the Colonial Sugar Refining Company. His social activities included theatre-going and the opera, and he was for many years associated with the Sydney Amateur Orchestral Society. For his many services to Australia, Charles Mackellar was knighted in 1912.

On March 7 1877 he proposed marriage to Marion, daughter of wealthy merchant, banker and pastoralist Thomas Buckland. Later the same day Marion replied:

MY DEAR DR MACKELLAR,

After much prayerful thought I have decided to say "*yes*" to the question you asked me this afternoon. May our dear Lord watch over you always and give you His peace which passeth all understanding is the prayers of

YRS VERY FAITHFULLY,
Marion Buckland
Belvoir House

Marion was direct, simple and fervent. Much of Charles Mackellar's personality is revealed in a letter written in 1892, at a time when the issue of voting rights was being heatedly debated:

Although the very mildest and timid of men, I become at times almost at the fighting point when I read and hear deliverances by birds of passage about our colony, our institutions, and ourselves. These men are clever, educated in a certain degree, *but not wise*. I have by long experience of men of various classes and degree learned to make a wide distinction between clever men and wise men, and I believe that there are some whom no education will make wise, and these "spouters" take advantage of the absence of wisdom in their hearers, to lead them on to perdition.

The ancient property qualification had this advantage, that it indicated in the voter or his father, energy to acquire, and prudence to keep. My views and expressions are now deemed heresy by the universal suffrage advocates, but I shall never hold other views; my friends say *I am too old to learn*.

Lady Mackellar,
c. 1900

Charles and Marion were married in 1877. Doubtless some of Charles Mackellar's commercial connections were due to the influence of his father-in-law, who for some years was president of the Bank of New South Wales as well as chairman of the board of the Colonial Sugar Refining Company until shortly before his death in 1896.

Following his marriage, Charles Mackellar built Dunara, a sandstone house of classic dignity overlooking the tranquil beauty of Rose Bay on Sydney Harbour. It was there that the third of his four children was born at 2.15 am on July 1 1885. Six weeks later the infant was baptised Isobel Dorothea Marion Mackellar. From babyhood she was known as Dorothea. Her elder brothers, Keith Kinnaird and Eric Buckland, were both born on July 17, in 1880 and 1882 respectively. With the birth of Malcolm on September 29 1889 the family was complete.

Sharing a habit later developed in turn by Dorothea, both Charles Mackellar and his wife used to jot down stray facts and *bon mots* on scraps of paper. For example:

> The secret of the wonderful success of the Scottish people, both mental and physical, lies in the fact that any nation trained to survive a diet of oatmeal and the shorter catechism could survive anything and flourish anywhere.

Charles also regularly worked out how much he was worth—a very considerable sum by 1900—and once a year Marion would note the height and weight of her children "measured on bare skin and bare feet". By the age of fourteen Dorothea was a healthy 8 stone 10 pounds, 5 feet 3½ inches tall, and 31 inches (34 inches when she inhaled) around the chest. She gazes confidently from photographs taken in her early teens, her rounded face full of thoughtful intelligence.

A few ephemeral glimpses of Dorothea Mackellar's childhood survive in letters she exchanged with her eldest brother, Keith, whose death in 1900 was the catastrophic event which inspired "When It Comes", her first recorded poem. The earliest letter is dated February 26 1891:

MY DEAR DOROTHEA,
        I hope you are quite well. How are the kittens, there are three down here. I have planted a little oak tree and Fritz has planted some acorns. I cannot think of any more to say so with love,

I AM YOUR LOVING BROTHER
KEITH

In subsequent letters Keith wrote to Dorothea about her pigeons and finches, of the pansies that "are out in your garden". By 1897 her governess was encouraging Dorothea to express herself in French. One letter begins:

MON CHÈRE KEITH,
        J'espère que tu recevras cette lettre vendredi avant tu partis pour l'école, parcequ'à moins ce n'est aucun profit pour toi et moi . . .

Two years later Charles Mackellar acquired the country property of Torryburn, reputed to be the inspiration for the verse about the breaking of the drought in "My Country", and located 160 kilometres north of Sydney, near Maitland. A letter dated July 5 1899, written by Keith to Dorothea at Torryburn, makes the first mention of a fantasy life which, in the light of what I was to find in her diaries, is revealing: ". . . What a splendid game this one of yours of talking, thinking and living in the Middle Ages must be . . ."

After completing his education at Sydney Grammar School, Keith enrolled at Sydney University and also took drawing lessons from the artist Anthony Dattilo-Rubbo. Both these pursuits were put aside when the Boer War began on October 12 1899. Keith enlisted in a New South Wales bush regiment and sailed for South Africa on January 25 1900. His first letter to Dorothea was optimistic, if somewhat bemused:

. . . It seems funny for me to have as my juniors men from ten to fifteen years my senior, doesn't it? I feel quite strange, as everything connected with this biz. does. Much as I miss you all, I am enjoying this life above everything I have ever experienced and feel sure that it is what I will do best at and that [*sic*]

not a Napoleon just yet though in future time I may be one, and in everything else I am an awful duffer. The men are in great spirits though thank goodness the other kind of spirits which get in them are not obtainable . . .

Soon after the despatch of this letter the Mackellar family left for England. They thought the war would end soon and planned a reunion with Keith in London. But by May 1900 the young soldier's dreams of glory had been discarded.

> . . . I expect that you are all enjoying England very much. I know that I shall be glad enough when this war is over—I'm pretty sick of it now, especially that we get heavy frost every night, they made sleeping in the open hardly what one might call fun. However it can't last much longer . . .

On June 18 Keith wrote what was to be his final letter. He complained that he had not received any letters from Dorothea since the family left for England:

> . . . That wretch De Vet [Christian de Wet, leader of the Boer guerilla troops] has captured and burnt all our mails which needless to say is an awful disappointment to us. Nearly all the men are now heartily sick of the war and wish they could finish the Boers off at one fell swoop and get home.
> *"Qua re facilus dicere quam facere est"*! I have some stamps and Kruger coins for you which in time will be valuable because they will be out of use. How you must be enjoying the wonderful sights and sounds of the new world in which you are now moving . . .

By the end of June 1900 Mafeking had been relieved and the war was all but over. All that remained, it was thought, was a little mopping up. The Mackellar family was jubilant. Then, on July 11 1900, and shortly before his 20th birthday, Keith Mackellar was killed at Onderstepoort. News of his death reached the family within days of their arrival in London, and Sydney newspapers reported it in full. According to the testimony of an unidentified member of the 1st Australian Horse, Keith had volunteered to take his troop to despatch a small number of Boers said to be hidden in a certain farmhouse. But the number was greater than anticipated, and Keith was the first to fall in the exchange of fire. The account continued:

Sir Charles Mackellar

> There was not a man in the regiment that did not admire and respect him . . . and when the coffin was lowered . . . there was not a man amongst us that did not have a struggle to stop the tears from coming . . .

OPPOSITE: Keith Mackellar

Charles Mackellar later received a more disturbing account of Keith's death, a report written by Colonel Donovan of the Cavalry Division:

> . . . On approaching the farm, an extensive property, some men were noticed moving about in khaki uniform and helmets. These were supposed to be patrols of the Hussar detachment. Lt. Mackellar and his men continued their course to the house, when suddenly at about 40 paces distant they were met by a murderous rifle fire. Lieut. Mackellar received a Mauser bullet wound in the forehead which instantly killed him. The villainous Boers had treacherously used our helmets and uniforms . . .

The family received hundreds of condolences, sad little black-edged letters, often in black-edged envelopes. Marion Mackellar was desperate, her grief heightened by a sense of outrage. Believing that the war was over, it had not occurred to her that her son's life might be at risk. The words of Dr Robert Scot-Skirving, a close friend of the family, give most touching expression to the sentiment of all who had known Keith:

> [Alexander] Macormick told me a day or two ago of the terrible loss you have sustained. It is no use chafing a sore by writing all I feel for you on the matter. Still I wish to tell you how deeply and lastingly I must always think on dear Keith—I liked the boy very, very much. A finer, pluckier lad I have never known. We all liked and respected him—brave, good-looking, wholesome-minded and honourable . . .

And Dorothea, aged fifteen, wrote a poem:

Dorothea's grandmother,
Isobel Mackellar

WHEN IT COMES

When would I like to die, to die?
Without a cry
In a hard-fought fight where blows are dealt
And the death-strokes less than a girl's kiss felt—
So would I die.

So would I like to die, but where?
On the open plain, in the open air,
Where the red blood soaks in the thirsty grass
And the wild things tread my grave as they pass—
There would I die.

When would I like to die? At night.
A moonless night.
The still white stars overhead
And underneath the still white dead.
Then would I die.

Deep and lasting though her grief at her brother's death eventually proved, Dorothea was at that time a lively and curious 15-year-old from Australia, and Europe must have seemed exciting. A few mementos of the visit show that, although the family decided to make an early return to Australia, they visited France in September. Dorothea kept a brochure from a Parisian exhibition, pasting it into her scrapbook with the comment: "It was much nicer than it looks, and I wish we had had more time. Statues splendid."

By December 1900 the family arrived home. Dorothea returned to a life she described as "sheltered" in the 1907 poem "Captive", surrounded by a small and clannish group which worked and played together, and in which with the passing of the years the lines between friendship and kinship blurred. But with Keith's death nothing was the same, and she regularly turned to the fantastic world of her own making referred to in Keith's letter of 1899. Her lively imagination gave birth to a number of entities, described in her diaries as "play-people", through whom she could experience emotions and experiences denied her in reality, and whose destinies she could control. Their life sagas began to unfold, month after month, year after year . . .

Dorothea's grandfather, Frederick Mackellar

In 1904 the family again travelled overseas—to Japan, North America, Europe and London. Dorothea continued to manipulate the lives of her "play-people", charting their changing fortunes in her "play-books" and encouraging her friends to enter her world of make-believe and act out her fantasies with her. Of all her alter-egos (and in 1910 54 were already in existence, complete with birthdays) one of the most beloved and constant, accompanying her for more than 20 years, was "Kid" Prevost. It was his name that she adopted when she wished to publish under a pseudonym. Destined to become the hero of her novel *Outlaw's Luck*, published in 1913 by Mills & Boon, "the Kid" epitomised the zenith of dash and derring-do. Perhaps in "the Kid" may be found an unconscious echo of Keith, the brother she loved and lost.

After another overseas visit in 1907, Charles Mackellar bought Kurrumbede, a 3650 hectare farm at Gunnedah, New South Wales, settling it on Eric and Malcolm in March 1909. There they raised Corriedale sheep, and Eric mastered the gentleman's sport of polo, which he had first played as a child with Keith in the grounds surrounding Dunara. Dorothea continued to live with her parents, by this time resident at 183 Liverpool Street, overlooking Hyde Park in the centre of Sydney. According to an interview given towards the end of her life, she attended lectures in Literature at Sydney University, though she was never formally enrolled as a student.

From 1907 her poems began to be published in newspapers and journals in Australia, England and America. Her parents were proud of her, Marion collecting each poem as it was published and carefully adding it to her scrapbook, and Charles sending copies to his friends as Christmas greetings. Yet though her work attracted attention and reviewers commented on her descriptive ability, sincerity and charm, a letter from the editor of the *Spectator* to Lady Poore, a literary patron, privately expressed some reservations:

> I had to send back some of her things today, simply because they were so rough in the execution, with extra or limping feet. One of them called "Burning Off" was really a splendid picture of burning trees at the Rampadells, I think the name was. If you should come across her, beg her to take more trouble with the form and finish, but encourage her to any extent, as she has real vision and a passionate love of nature.

But publication of her work did not bring her full satisfaction. With her brothers now living away from home, she began to kick against the restrictions life imposed on her. One long poem from early 1907 begins:

> *They say that women's lives are only Love*
> *That naught else really counts, that we must wait*
> *For that fulfilment. It is well, but yet —*
> *Would I might go and bathe me at the Spring*
> *Of all romance—I'd act instead of dream . . .*
> *Heavens! The things I'd do, were I a man.*

And in "Captive", she writes:

> *My soul is sick of the soft slow days.*
> *My heart is sick of the gentle ways.*
> *My body sick of its silken thrall.*
> *Sick—I am sick to death of it all!*

I would go—it is not so far
Close to the earth where the gipsies are,
Where good and evil lie bare to sight
In full discomfort and full delight.

You need not tell me my woman's heart
Would quail and shrink at the evil part,
I know that true and I know the cost —
But the gain would pay me for what I lost!

Do you suppose that I have not thought
How I would regret this sheltered port?
—Not in the storm and the fierce hot stress
But in sick calms and in loneliness.

There's some trouble whenever you go —
I would regret this, but I would know
Saint or devil—or slug or star,
Hail to the God of Things as They Are!

Whilst the mythology surrounding "My Country" has it that Dorothea was 18 or 19 when it was written, her constancy in recording her verses at the time of writing leads me to suspect that it was written shortly after "Captive", when she was 22. "Core of My Heart", as entered in her verse book in the first weeks of 1908, was clearly an early draft, and several changes were made before its publication later that year.

The poetry of that time also reflects her parents' hope that she would marry: all their preparation equipped her, not for a career, but for marriage. Under the watchful gaze of a chaperone, she had taken her place as a young socialite, attending the events which might lead to a romance.

I had already begun transcribing the diaries when I was contacted by Adrienne Matzenik. She kindly elaborated on the stories contained in her introduction to *My Country and Other Poems of Dorothea Mackellar.* She believed that Dorothea had twice been engaged, the first time in 1908, and again in 1914.

Her understanding of events concerning the first engagement, as related to her by Dorothea at the end of her life, is that Dorothea ended the relationship after her fiancé (never named by Dorothea) objected to her staying with the family of Sir William MacGregor, Governor of Queensland, at a time when the American Fleet was visiting Brisbane.

It appears that, in her talks to her nurse, Dorothea may have been rewriting history. I could find no evidence of an engagement for Dorothea in 1908 and, in any case, Sir William MacGregor did not live in Australia until he assumed the governorship of Queensland in December 1909. Dorothea's diaries show that she did visit the MacGregors, in June 1910, but the visit was not preceded by a broken romance.

Adrienne Matzenik also spoke of Dorothea's second "romance", with Patrick Chalmers—a beautiful love story that has appeared in print on a number of occasions in recent years. During a visit to London, so the story goes, Dorothea had met and fallen in love with Patrick Reginald Chalmers (who, incidentally, in his poetry collection *Green Days and Blue Days* gave the world the line "What's lost on the roundabouts, we pulls up on the swings"). Following Patrick's proposal of marriage, she returned to Australia in order that her parents could announce the engagement. However, by then the Great War had begun. They lost touch with each other, and in 1919, eager to discover whether or not he had survived the war, she returned to London to find—to her great sorrow—that he had recently married another.

Dorothea certainly knew and liked Patrick Chalmers, but, as the diaries made clear, there was no romantic attachment, and they occasionally corresponded throughout the war years. I came to the inescapable conclusion that these stories were Dorothea's inventions in old age, and served to satisfy a credulous listener, curious why she never married.

I could see that there was a strand of fact running through Dorothea's tales, and possibly the story of an engagement in 1908 was inspired by events that happened to Eric. In 1908 he had proposed to one of Dorothea's close friends, Dorothy, daughter of the barrister Henry Owen. The Owens did not agree to the marriage, and a heated exchange of letters took place between Mrs Owen and Mrs Mackellar, which culminated in each accusing the other's offspring of being a danger to their own. Dorothea went to see Mrs Owen, hoping to soothe her, but, she afterwards reported, "Mrs Owen gave me her hand, looking out of the window". Lady Mackellar eventually kept Mrs Owen's letters in a large envelope, sealed not once but repeatedly and haphazardly, with black sealing wax.

If I was initially disappointed at not finding evidence of the romance of Dorothea and Patrick in the diaries, I found another relationship that was more unusual and intriguing: Dorothea's association with Ruth Bedford. In Ruth she found not only a friend with whom she could share the labour of writing two novels, but someone who eagerly embraced her secret life.

Dorothea first met Ruth in London in 1904, though it was not until the early days of 1910, when Ruth entered Dorothea's existence like the proverbial "breath of fresh air", that they became close friends. There were many parallels in their lives: Australians of similar age (Ruth was three years older) and upbringing, they shared a love of writing. Ruth's plain exterior concealed a quick wit and a sympathetic, romantic nature. The story of their friendship and their unusual response to the limits imposed on women of their class in Australia in the early decades of this century became one of the most engrossing aspects of the diaries.

Mackellar family at Dunara, c. 1900

I had based the libretto of the opera *Dorothea* on the romance between Patrick and Dorothea, and for a while it seemed as if I would have to find another motif for the opera. Then I recognised that the story, with its escapism from reality, characterised much that I had come to know of Dorothea through her diaries. In the conflict between fantasy and reality, I had found the drama I needed.

Long before the work of transcribing the diaries was complete, it was evident that they would need to be substantially reduced for purposes of publication. I have, therefore, omitted many passages devoted to lunches, teas, dinners, plays, books, hair-washings, weather reports and acting. Nothing has been omitted that could permit a false interpretation of events, nor have I engaged in censorship. Some long descriptive passages have been abridged, and, in a very few cases, a word or two has been changed for purposes of clarification. Many entries in the diaries ended with a series of dots, indicating either a trailing away of thought or something left unsaid. To avoid confusion with the ellipses which I have inserted to indicate omissions, this is now indicated with a dash. Names abridged by Dorothea have sometimes been spelled out, to avoid intrusive square brackets. Her occasional quirks of spelling are retained. By comparing the diaries with her verse books, it has been possible to include certain poems, previously unpublished. Many other poems referred to in the text have, of course, been published, most recently in *My Country and Other Poems of Dorothea Mackellar.*

The jigsaw I have endeavoured to put together still has missing pieces, but I hope that with the publication of Dorothea Mackellar's diaries some light, at least, will be shed on the woman who made Australia "a sunburnt country". I am indebted to the staff of the Mitchell Library, especially John Murphy; to Jenya Osborne, Dorothea Hedger, Helen Rutledge, Reg Broun, Diane Levy, Stanley Ciccone and Denis Condon for practical assistance and information; to Sue Phillips, my editor, for her perceptive comments and for her idea of presenting the diaries in illustrated form; to Alan Holley for his stoic support; and most of all to Kath Strang, to whom my work is dedicated with love.

JYOTI BRUNSDON
Sydney 1988

OPPOSITE: Dorothea, *c.* 1910

For Sport, for Dress, for Business
HENDERSON HATS
meet every requirement.

At Home and Away 1910-11

- *Chased by black swans* • *Moonlit walk* • *Reading* The Green Carnation
- *Motoring to Medlow in a Clement Talbot* • *Serious love at 11.30 in a bathing house!*
- *The King is dead—town hung with half-masted flags* •

183 LIVERPOOL STREET, SYDNEY

In January 1910 Dorothea Mackellar was 24 years old and lived with her parents in a large apartment overlooking Hyde Park in the centre of Sydney. Her life, as a member of the city's social elite, was privileged but restricted. She enjoyed the privileges and, before long, a secret life provided some escape from the restrictions.

Church . . . Lunch in room and wrapper. Seaward.* Strong north-easter. Sat in corner of garden. Looked at porcelain books and tried on hats. Two of them I love and covet greatly . . . Gradually getting verses typed again. I wonder if it will ever come to anything?

Sunday January 2

Worked a little ("Vespers"—it won't come straight) . . . Cooked with the chafing dish—only salted almonds, but they are very successful. Tailor and dressmaker. Very hot . . . Rested in the Domain . . .

Tuesday January 4

. . . Read *Lord Leonard the Luckless* and *Audrey the Actress* for Bush Book Club.* *L.L.L.* utter drivel. Audrey (what play memories!*) has points, but writing's hardly the author's profession . . .

Friday January 7

Got silk handkerchief to bathe in (sounds inadequate) . . . Tidied room and

Saturday January 8

Seaward: The Point Piper home of Dorothea's godmother, Florence Binnie.

Club: Bush Book Club (BBC), founded in 1909. For over 40 years it supplied books to people in remote areas of NSW.

memories!: From childhood Dorothea had invented plays. The plots, with their myriad of play-people and acts, were written down and the dialogue was spontaneously improvised with a friend.

changed photographs and ornaments in it. Felt too tired to go out . . . Evening: Played with Mother, bed early. Much later heard Dad come home after the banquet with Lord Kitchener.* Got up and snuggled on him and heard about things.

Tuesday January 11

. . . It rained. Ruth Bedford and Mimi came. I couldn't talk to either and Mimi rubbed me up, though she is a dear really. The family were awfully nice, but I felt horribly ill. Went to bed early and could not sleep.

Friday January 14

Florence came, frightfully worried. **Her pretty maid Cayley has just had a child** . . .

Saturday January 15

. . . Very hot steamy day . . . Made toffee and didn't boil it long enough . . . Played with Mac [brother Malcolm] and toffee . . .

Monday January 17

Went to Dr Bennet* and the old fraud kept me waiting for ages . . . He insisted on giving me a tonic—and I feel perfectly well . . . Evening: Typed, tried to write about Murmur [brother Eric's greyhound] . . .

LIVERPOOL ST. — NATIONAL PARK

Tuesday January 18

. . .Rushed off to Florence at National Park. It was looking just beautiful. Sat on the lawn and **smoked to keep the mosquitoes away**. Very tired. Worked hard to soothe Florence. She is very jumpy. No wonder.

Wednesday January 19

Breakfasted in our wrappers on the veranda, lazed nearly all the morning . . . Afternoon: Bathed. F. didn't. The walk to the bathing place is pretty, and it's rather nice too. Very big, but lots of shallow. I kept to the far end. There was nobody there but two very small girls who didn't go out of their depth. Evening: F. talked of her worry, which I think did her good.

Thursday January 20

. . . Scorching hot day. Remained in our kimonos all the morning, read and yarned. There is nobody here but us . . . Afternoon: Walked up the river road.

Lord Kitchener: Commander-in-Chief of British forces in South Africa, Viscount Kitchener was in Australia for defence discussions.
Bennet: Dr Francis Bennet, specialist in skin diseases.

F.'s little dog Koti is really rather a duck, he's such a little sport.
Evening: Talked in the dark—we fairly live on the veranda.
But the mosquitoes—*pajaritos infernales*! [hellish little
fliers] I never knew anything like them.

Friday January 21

Hired a boat and rowed far up the river. It was
delicious. Everything is looking beautiful, and the
black swans chased us and begged for bits of apple.
We got home just before the rain began—an awful storm
which lasted all the afternoon. We watched in comfort and
content from the veranda. This place never looks alike for two
hours together . . . F. seems much better.

Saturday January 22

. . . My shoulders are dreadfully burnt, I feel like a flayed
martyr. We were going fishing, but are scared by the quantities of fish you're
liable to catch. It's a five pound penalty if they're the wrong length—and we
had no tape measure! Evening: Lovely moonlit walk up the hill. Dear little
rock wallabies quite tame. F. very poetic and Koti a mighty hunter.

Swarms of people here . . . Another walk up the hill, but the people had scared
the wallabies (who came there with their children) and F. was nervous.
(**Irritable, poor dear**) The moon was beyond reproach. We do feel so much
better.

*Sunday
January 23*

The following day Dorothea returned home.

. . . Dressmaker and a little shopping. Got 2nd-hand Violet Fairy Book with
beautiful coloured Ford pictures. Sat in gardens with Mother and read. Lovely.
Eric has lost no stock by this awful flood, but he has had a terribly anxious

*Tuesday
January 25*

time.* Mac is with him now . . . Sir Normand* and Dr. McC.* came to dinner. Both dears. Sir Normand very gay and charming . . .

Wednesday January 26

Wrote to Will Masefield thanking him for "The Squatter's Lament"* and to many others . . . Evening: Typed till rather late, tho' Dad thought I had gone to bed and locked me out, and I had to climb in over the partition as the back door was locked too. I felt like a Prodigal Son; it was rather nice.

Friday January 28

It *poured*: so I did not go to the BBC. I read for it and wrote a little . . . and lazed. Afternoon: Dressmaker and Ruth Bedford. Nice, good talk. Pretty, rainy day . . .

I like Ruth.

Tuesday February 1

. . . Reading *The Green Carnation*, which is clever in spots, but very wearisome. That sort of thing gets old-fashioned so soon. Afternoon: . . . Got nice and sinfully expensive gold shoes . . . Evening: Dell Milne and I went to *The Merry Widow*. I love it—I do wish I could have seen Lily Elsie as Sonia! But it *is* hefty—We enjoyed ourselves.

Friday February 4

Bathe at Rose Bay Baths with Florence. Lesson from Farmer in scissors-kick. Rather to my surprise he said I swam breast-stroke in very good style. But the scissors-kick *is* hard! I tried treading water too. It's not so difficult as I thought. Afternoon: Big BBC meeting at Lockleys [Library in Martin Place]. Lady Poore* in chair—sweet as usual. I was so sleepy. I couldn't even write a letter when I got home . . .

Tuesday February 8

. . . Father came back. He says the results of the flood are awful.

time: Eric and Malcolm's property Kurrumbede was situated on the Namoi River at Gunnedah, 450 kilometres north-west of Sydney.
Normand: Sir Henry Normand MacLaurin, surgeon, Chancellor of the University of Sydney and a director of the Bank of New South Wales.
McC.: Sir Alexander McCormick, eminent surgeon and yachtsman.
"The Squatter's Lament": The poem, by Ted Brooks, includes the couplet: "The woolly lamb/It rhymes with damn."
Lady Poore: Wife of Admiral Sir Richard Poore, who served in Australia 1908–11.

OPPOSITE: *The Garden Bench* Rupert Bunny

... Talked to Dad about committees and managing people—wish I was out of the Norland [Sydney Norland Institute Loan Fund Committee] without the fight for getting out!

Was going to a beastly meeting when Bertha* rang up to say that Mr Nicholas* wanted me to go and hear the Bowling trial* (conspiracy)—so after a short debate I chucked it, feeling guilty, but I'm not sorry. The trial was awfully interesting. Mr Gannon spoke of poor dark old England and sunny NSW and so on, but he's clever for all that ... Evening: Went to Bertha and jigsawed a pretty Lady Hamilton.

LIVERPOOL ST. — MEDLOW

Friday February 11

... Motored to Medlow in a Clement Talbot with the Parents, Dr August Scheidel and a Shover [chauffeur] with a nice voice. But unfortunately his mouth is always open. It was a lovely day **but I would rather not have had to talk so much**.

Dear Mountains! Hydro Majestic childishly magnificent and tawdry ...

MEDLOW — PORTLAND

Saturday February 12

The dear men hurried us up much earlier than was necessary! and we went to Lithgow and saw a blast furnace (Hoskin's). It was a marvellous sight. First the slag ran out like a terrible gold snake, and then the iron, red and gold and apricot ... Then we came to Portland and Dr Scheidel showed us over

---

Bertha: Dorothea's friend Bertha Brady, daughter of Andrew Brady, Sydney's leading ear specialist.
Nicholas: Harold Nicholas, barrister and writer, later judge. Unsuccessful attempts were made at one time to "match-make" between Harold Nicholas and Dorothea. In spite of this, their shared love of theatre ensured a continuing friendship.
trial: Australia was in the grip of a coal strike. Strike-leader Peter Bowling and four others refused to accept arbitration ruling, were found guilty of conspiracy and given heavy gaol sentences.

his works till we literally dropped. But I loved them too—the huge quarries and the revolving kilns and the 18,000 h.p. plant and the flying fox and the caterpillar. The furnaces are magnificent at night. We dressed in long coats and felt hats 'cause of the dust. There is a splendid band, too—mostly employees.

PORTLAND — SYDNEY

. . . Lunched at Katoomba . . . Dr Scheidel is awfully kind, but he does get on my nerves . . . *Home.* Good to be home. I feel as if I have been away a month.

Sunday February 13

Went for a bathe at Rose Bay. There was no one there and it was heavenly. The water was clear as a green crystal . . . Afternoon: Shopped. Saw about brown evening dress . . . Ruth here. Good talk, on the roof, and I got her to stay to dinner and yarned about Indian history and Plays—and we're going to try acting together! Went over Prevost Play.* I was *so excited* afterwards that I couldn't sleep.

Monday February 14

. . . Met Jim Fairfax* and I like him. He wouldn't talk anything but poetry and publishers to me. I expect he thinks I don't like anything else . . .

Tuesday February 15

Bathed, had another lesson. I think I'm getting the hang of it. Wrote to D.O.* **(It's uphill work nowadays)** . . . It was a hot night, but I'm not feeling it at all. It makes one seem rather heartless when others do so much.

Thursday February 17

. . . Went to poor Florence. She is having her nose and throat done. Talked awhile. She tries to be cheerful. Met Ruth. Wrote a little of the story she wanted me to—It won't sell.

Friday February 18

Bathed with Ruth . . . I'm getting on slowly with the trudgeon stroke . . .

Saturday February 19

Play: C. L. "Kid" Prevost was a favourite play character and, later, the subject of her novel *Outlaw's Luck.* Born in a rectory in the north of Ireland, the Kid went to live in South America, where he fell under the sway of the masterful Urquiza until rescued by beautiful Katherine Hammond . . .
Fairfax: James Griffyth Fairfax, poet and a member of the influential Sydney family of newspaper proprietors. Dorothea sometimes refers to him as "Mr. Jim".
D.O.: For some years Dorothy Owen was Dorothea's acting companion. The friendship foundered in 1908 when Dorothy's parents refused to let her marry Eric Mackellar.

Bathed with Ruth—floated in great ease and comfort and *tried* to dive. Ver' moosin' . . . Afternoon: Hardy's (lovely opal necklace) and M. got nice grey hat . . . Evening: Father and I went to *The Fencing Master*. It's a fairly obvious comedy drama . . . Grace* looked lovely, and was a dear.

Meeting of Sydney Home for Babies at Waverly. (Rather lofty old house with pillared foundations. Would have been gorgeous for acting.) Trying and protracted meeting, during which I spoke my mind and announced that I was going to resign. I really didn't do it badly and no one had a chance of objecting. Thank Heaven it is over! They were quite nice about it. Scrappy lunch and Sewing Meeting, over which *I* presided, Merciful Powers! Rather funny. Evening: Dead tired. Wrote a little.

Went with Ruth to bathe at Bondi and couldn't till 12.30—the surf was so glorious too! So we paddled, and R. was nearly swept away and drenched from top to toe. We dried ourselves on a hot flat rock *and-we-acted-the Prevost Play*! I think it was so courageous in cold blood on a salt morning. Really rather successful . . . Afternoon: Shopping, and I discovered my Boggabri story going the rounds of the American magazines, and they had illustrated it with a black bushman attired in leaves!—lovely. Evening: Wrote "The Lie".*

Ruth came *and* we acted. I have never been fuller of electricity. We did her Barbara and my Japanese girl—on the roof. It *was* good.

. . . Dined with the Charlie Fairfaxes. It was a nice, young dinner and after the others had settled down to bridge, Mr Jim and I went into the billiard room and he showed me his manuscript books and the new Lionel Lindsay etchings for the next one that is to be published. They are really beautiful— such trees and clouds! . . . Home at 12 p.m.

Grace: Grace Palotta, friend of Dorothea, and an actress renowned for her beauty.
"The Lie": A short story later published in *Southern Sphere* under the pen-name C. L. Prevost.

OPPOSITE: *Untitled Beach Scene* Roy de Maistre

Friday *March 4*	Wrote "Coorong Sandhills" and copied some things . . . Evening: a lot of Orchestrelle.*
Tuesday *March 8*	. . . Opening of Mitchell Library. Very interesting. Lord Chelmsford [Governor of New South Wales 1909-13] made a nice speech. Horrid pain in eye. Did more secretary work and lay down in the dark. Telephoned in the evening, wildly and successfully. I think Ruth will come tomorrow. (Our last chance of acting for some time.)
Wednesday *March 9*	Wrote about Dryads and things. It went very well, but I didn't finish . . . Ruth came. I told her the Prevost idea and we acted George and Kozakura. Then tea—and Mr Cochrane and Mrs Leslie. I was glad to see them, but it did shorten the afternoon . . . Bertha came in the evening. She is a dear darling. She will have to wear glasses, which is very sad. I hope it won't be for long. She made me show her verses. I was shy and I don't think she liked 'em much—I don't wonder after Jim's.
Thursday *March 10*	**Flopped.** Read a little and made lace. Meg* came . . . It was nice to have her again. Just talk . . .
Friday *March 11*	**Pain pretty bad in spite of the cachets** . . . Molly Merivale came. She's young and cruel—she'll be old herself some day and oh, she *will* hate it so! Evening: Dad went away, taking my throat pastilles and leaving me two shillings to get more. They're 2/6d but he hadn't a saxpence! Bless him. Talked about lots of things—Birth and Death and so on —
Saturday *March 12*	Felt very limp. Wrote a little and read. Lunched with Mr McPhillamy at the Australia . . . It simply *poured.* We went home soon, Lili, Meg and I, and yarned till supper . . . The girls had to go out. I was sorry, but it was a nice evening all the same. It's fun being different people! "I love acting", as Mr Charles Emerson said long ago.

Orchestrelle: A grand Victorian instrument which combines the characteristics of a player piano with those of an harmonium. In 1909 Charles Mackellar insured his orchestrelle for £200.

Meg: Meg McPhillamy, member of a prominent Bathurst family. Meg and her sister Lili were childhood friends of Dorothea, and Meg's friendship was to last a lifetime.

Went swimming with Meg & Ruth. It was raining and we had the baths to ourselves, so after about an hour I grabbed my resolution with both hands and got Farmer to give me a diving lesson. It was detestable at first, my knees would *not* give way; it is much easier to jump than to fall. But I did improve! It was really fun. Never so bad again . . .

. . . Norland Loan Fund Ball meeting—ugh. Afternoon: Called with Mother. No luck, everyone was in, but I *was* glad to see Mrs Charlie Fairfax, looking exactly like a violet in a plain dark purple dress with lovely pearls and an amethyst . . .

. . . Shopping. Saw nice three-cornered hat, black with a gold quill, and wanted it very much. Evening: Theatre with the girls and Mr Bean.* It was great fun and two rats made a diversion in the gallery. I love Oscar Asche—N.B. The marriage customs of the Greeks are: each man has only one wife and this is called Monotony.

Lili, I'm sorry to say, went away by the morning train. I wrastled with the Customs, quite successfully, and then had a fitting. The English dress is a pretty dull green and dull silver thing, with Ninon paniers, very soft, and a silver rose. I love it . . . Evening: Yarned and read and yarned. Read some of Moratin's comedies. They are awfully good. He must have been considered such a daring modernist in what he says about women.

. . . Ruth and I went out to Diamond Bay,* picnicking. It was a heavenly day and there were heaps of mauve and white violets. I told her about Pearl and Charlie,* then we acted Kid Prevost's saga for hours. The landscape *did* fit in! It was too good for words. The feeling is on me still, I can't think myself free of the play. It went awfully well. Oh that sun-soaked *cañon*! She loved it too. Evening: Sleepy and happy. Early bed.

I'm still Kid! It feels so funny—I can't leave off — . . . Charlie Bean's launch party, up Lane Cove. Mr Jose* told me some interesting things about . . . Kipling.

Bean: Charles Bean, journalist, later war correspondent and historian. Dorothea also refers to him as Charlie, C.B. and C.E.W.B.
Diamond Bay: A rugged ocean bay at Vaucluse.
Charlie: Dorothea's cousin Pearl Faithfull had just become engaged to Charles Wentworth Dilke.
Jose: Arthur Jose, journalist and historian.

I never saw such ankles as his wife's. Elephants aren't in it . . . Evening: Meg went to the theatre. I typed and waited up for her. Then we talked far too late on various grave problems. We talk boldly, but we are afraid.

Monday March 21

Rain, but we went for a bathe, trying in vain to buy the black hat first. The bathe was scrumptious and quite private. We tried to dance in the water and sank . . .

Tuesday March 22

Got black hat . . . Went with Dad to reception of Japanese officers at Parliament House . . . Met the Flag Captain and others—heaps, but was in a fever to get away as Ruth was waiting for me. She did come and we acted, Carol and Kid—oh *dear*; they have fallen in love and they are so horribly unsuited! . . .

Wednesday March 23

Went bathing. It was lovely and I dived off the spring-board without minding. Hurrah! The worst is over . . . Got home in good time, went to the opening of the Easter Show . . . and a large intoxicated horseman insisted on making love* to me, which was embarrassing. I think it was that green silk coat that did it . . .

Monday March 28

Saw Meg off. Missed her horribly, though I did my best not to Brood. It was a lovely Aprilish day, but I couldn't get a chaperon for the races . . . Evening: Went unexpected-like to *As You Like It* with the Parents. Awfully nice . . .

Tuesday March 29

. . . Norland meeting. Went for a blessed bathe afterwards, all alone, and dived from the springboard. I'm going to try a running dive next . . .

Friday April 1

Ruth in the afternoon—at her house. Talked and acted a little of Kid's play. It *was* nice, but I want to act someone else now, I'm getting to be too much Kid. Evening: Australian Club Ball—decorated with red poppies. Beautiful, though

love: When Dorothea uses the phrases "making love" and "to make love", she is referring to amorous attention.

I hashed my programme like any debutante. Mixed and missed no less than *four* dances. Luckily there were swarms of people . . . Bed 3.15 a.m.

. . . Dentist (ever so much to do). Got 21 books for the BBC from A & R's [Angus & Robertson]. Rather nice ones. Called with Mother, most successfully. Nearly everyone out . . .

*Wednesday
April 6*

Felt ill, and couldn't go to Ball meeting . . . Wrote a little.

*Friday
April 8*

SMALL MERCIES

*Today I have an ache in my
    back and a plaguey cold in my head,
Neuralgia and a throbbing throat,
    and I ought to settle to bed,
But if I weren't on the sofa here
    I'd be taking minutes instead—*
Miserere Domine!

*So here I lie not an atom depressed,
    for is it not clear and plain
It's nicer far to read Chesterton
    in the complicatedest pain
Than to sit up in the smug Town Hall
    with those squabbling women again?*
Deo Gratias!

Stayed in bed all day. It appears it's ptomaine poisoning and Father has it too. It really feels beastly. Read a little and slept a lot . . .

*Saturday
April 9*

Morning entirely spent in rushes between the Town Hall and the Railway Station— I don't love those two places in spite of what they mean . . . Afternoon: Greta Morrison's wedding. Pretty yellow bridesmaids' dresses, yellow and brown. Sounds hideous, but it wasn't . . .

*Tuesday
April 12*

Polling day. There was a muddle about me at the booths, but I succeeded in voting . . . Caught tram to Rose Bay and met Ruth. She had written an awfully

*Wednesday
April 13*

nice thing about the Babies on the Roof*—I like it. Bathed, acting the Enchanted Island* (it *is* good to be absurd like that!) . . . and wasted a tram most scandalously. A letter was waiting for me, from the Champion.* I *shall* send things to him—Prosit! Evening: . . . Out to see the Election Results* . . . Exciting—a huge and good-tempered crowd.

Friday . . . Prepared MSS. for the Champion.
April 15

Saturday . . . Glorious day. I'm getting up a good deal of pace in that overarm
April 16 stroke . . . Evening: Finished MSS. Idled over old books.

Friday . . . Wild scurry to buy soda water and collapsible cups at Mark Foys, and after
April 22 six departments had to go to Horderns. Missed tram and lost cups! However, I met Ruth at Ocean Street. Good bathe. Beautiful at Diamond Bay. We picnicked on olives and breadbutter and salted almonds and climbed down to the foot of the cliff and acted the Islanders, and a little of the Saga. Then the rain came pouring on. I rescued my silk coat (almost! I did love it so and I think it's spoilt). We took refuge in a small wet cave over a running stream and began the new play! Then I went to tea with Florence and home in her dress. Mine was dripping wet . . .

Roof: Dorothea often retreated to the privacy of the roof at home. After spending time there with Dorothea, Ruth had written twelve verses inscribed: "To the Other Baby (Damned bad lines in return for a beautiful evening)", two of which read:

> *One is more than common wise,*
> *One too grave for youth.*
> *Both would raise unflinching eyes*
> *To the eyes of Truth.*
>
> *Yet the land of Let's Pretend*
> *Opens for them wide;*
> *Here is life that has no end,*
> *Here is love untried.*

The Enchanted Island: One of Dorothea's plays.
Champion: Henry Hyde Champion, journalist, publisher, social propagandist and founder of the Australasian Authors' Agency. Often referred to as H.H.C.
Results: The federal election resulted in a commanding majority for the Labor Party.

Meant to go for a swim, but Mrs Brady asked me to go to the Commemoration.* Did heaps of telephoning, scribbled a little, and went. Got excellent seat (through Mrs Barraclough). The students made a nice noise, but it's a blackguardly thing to interrupt an old man as they did. Sir Normand was awfully angry. I don't wonder. Lord Chelmsford spoke *very* well. He got in one good dig too.*

Saturday April 30

Dentist. He kept me waiting an awful time, but showed me good snapshots of Houdini flying. Revised verses. Went and lunched at the Kiosk with Ruth (such a funny little place, with a distinct flavour of "irrespectability for girls") and afterwards to the Art Gallery, to act Antony* and incidentally to see the new picture Las Mantillas Negras. It's good. *All* was good . . .

Monday May 2

Ruth came unexpectedly—joy! We acted Tony and his Italian lady, which was really rather clever of us. Serious love at 11.30 in a bathing house! It went quite well, but Ruth wouldn't cut the interview short and we were awfully late! I couldn't, being a Perfect Gentleman. Afternoon: Vera Simpson's wedding. Very nice . . .

Wednesday May 4

Dentist. Long and beastly . . . Shopped. Got the beautiful tortoiseshell pins that Eric gave me, and a pretty lace-pin. And stockings of divers hues — . . .

Thursday May 5

. . . Dentist (worse than yesterday) . . . Paid bills and cashed *Bulletin* and *Sunday Times* postal notes—and got motor bonnet from the Customs on paying a heavy duty—and it's a vile and poisonous green that I wouldn't wear for a kingdom. *Very* disappointing, when I sent the pattern and all . . . Evening: Stage Society. *The Cassilis Engagement* . . . Ruth came and we were just longing to act Tony (we did in the intervals). We wanted to stay at home and do it but felt it wouldn't be decent.

Friday May 6

Commemoration: Commemoration Day at Sydney University was always a rowdy event. On this particular occasion it also celebrated the 25th anniversary of the granting of full academic rights to women, and it was reported that the Chancellor, Sir Normand MacLaurin, "was so completely interrupted that after a strong appeal to the undergraduates he left more than half his address unread . . . One student devoted undivided attention to a cornet . . ." (*Sydney Morning Herald*, May 2 1910)
too: Lord Chelmsford's speech contained several "digs", including: "With the experience of 16 years of married life . . . I have come to realize that perfection is one of those things that the mind of man cannot comprehend."
Antony: Also known as Tony, the half-French boy hero of Dorothea's play The Little Blue Devil. Later the subject of the novel of the same name co-written with Ruth.

. . . At one o'clock today we looked out and saw the town hung with half-masted flags. The King is dead. It is horribly sudden.

Saturday
May 7

Wrote a little. Horribly gloomy day—weather and mourning together . . .

Monday
May 9

Dentist(‼) Wrote letters and play-letters* . . . Sat with Dad till 4, then went to dentist again . . . I'll be worn out soon! It makes me feel sick to get into that chair . . .

Thursday
May 12

Went to tidy up and found letter asking me to go with the McGregors* on their Northern Tour! Glory! . . .

Tuesday
May 17

Charles Bean wants to get me a publisher*—

Sunday
May 22

. . . Dentist—really excrutiating pain, but it's *over*. Hallelujah! . . . Wrote a very, very little. Early bed.

Monday
May 23

. . . Shopped till we could see our own sins. Got lovely black sequinned scarf, filmy and clinging as a snakeskin, and other things . . .

Wednesday
May 25

. . . Town—and cousin Lilian [Anderson]. She **is in trouble—I do wish I could do something, but it is money,** and that's always so difficult. Saw her off at station. Evening: Calve concert with Dad. *Splendid*. She did Carmen's duet from the second act, and a Cavalleria thing—and oh, lots . . . I liked Gasparri, the tenor, too—he sang beautifully, among other things a delightful Tuscan *canzona* that has haunted me ever since —

Thursday
May 26

play-letters: The correspondence between the characters in Ruth and Dorothea's plays. Both women became fond of writing and receiving "play-letters", often lengthy epistles containing the minutiae of the play-people's lives and travels, which they sent through the post in the normal way.
McGregors [*sic*]: Sir William MacGregor, Governor of Queensland, and family. Dorothea spells the name "McGregor" throughout.
publisher: Since 1907 Dorothea's poetry had appeared in Australian, English and American newspapers and journals. Charles Bean, who took a great interest in her work, encouraged her to find a publisher for a first anthology.

Friday *May 27*	Went to Dr Bennet's. Translated that *canzona** . . . Lunch. Dressmaker. Shopping. Attempt (failing disastrously) at tennis. My ankles gave way and my head began furiously to ache. I think it was sheer knock-up—
Saturday *May 28*	. . . Joined Ruth and went to Diamond Bay. Quite unexpectedly it was a lovely day, but I did not dare go down to the sea because my foot hurt so. However we were happy on top. We acted the Little Blue Devil,* a scene of the Enchanted Island, and a new phase of Kid's Saga, all at our leisure. Such a good day. We came back to Watson's Bay across the starry black harbour . . .
Sunday *May 29*	Church. Lovely morning. After breakfast I dried my washed hair on the roof, and the sky was just like some huge forgetmenot. Wrote play-letters. Afternoon: The Mackellars called on the MacLaurins. It's a pathetic womanless household* . . .

After three days of "strenuous" shopping, Dorothea was at last ready for her visit to Queensland. Her host, Sir William MacGregor, and Charles Mackellar were old friends, possibly since their student days in Scotland, though they had studied at different universities. After working for some years as a doctor, William MacGregor had accepted the first of many government posts of increasing importance in the Seychelles, Mauritius, Fiji, New Guinea and, as Governor, in Lagos and Newfoundland. The two men had kept in touch, and Charles Mackellar was delighted when Sir William was appointed Governor of Queensland in 1909.

The "Northern Tour" of Queensland, the highlight of which was to be the opening of the Carnival at Rockhampton, was Sir William's first official visit to the region. In addition to his wife and staff, his younger daughter, Mary, affectionately known as "Babs", was to accompany him. Dorothea was invited to join the tour as a companion for Babs.

canzona: Published with the title "Non Penso a Lei" in her collection *Witch-Maid* (J.M. Dent & Sons, 1914).
The Little Blue Devil: Dorothea's play about Tony.
household: Lady MacLaurin, mother of five sons, had died in 1908.

SYDNEY — TRAIN

. . . Bitterly cold, windy day . . . Dad (dear Dad) saw me off. Soon I felt horribly faint and ill, and cold as ice. Mr Metcalfe got me a large brandy and I went to bed, and thought of Mother and the play-people and an absurd letter of H.H.C.'s that amazed and puzzled me.

Friday
June 3

TRAIN — GOVT. HOUSE BRISBANE

Woke up in New England, going through miles and miles of snow. Rather interesting journey, but the Queensland trains do rock so. The last part after Toowoomba was so rough, I was awfully tired. Captain Hugh Scarlett was waiting at 10 p.m. with a long modern edition of Cinderella's coach (45 h.p. Mercedes, red leather), and I got in and was stared at through the glass while he saw about luggage. They were dears to me. I love Sir William, but I'm shy.

Saturday
June 4

. . . Lay on sofa by fire and studied Mme. de Thebes' palmistry book with Babs and found I'm a cross between a Jupiterienne and a Solère! . . .

Sunday
June 5

GOVT. HOUSE — TRAIN

. . . Packed. Waited. Went to station. So-o cold. Train very late. Nice private car, with people staring very hard through the glass, worse than on Saturday, of course.

Monday
June 6

TRAIN — ROCKHAMPTON
Tuesday June 7

Getting warmer and warmer, praise be. Breakfast at Bundaberg — bananas and palms growing more common, tawny grass and very green gum trees and others unknown. Mayor waiting at Rockhampton and children with

bouquets. My first conquest—Funny. Pretty town, splendid hills and nice river. The train runs right through the streets . . . (The child with the purple orchids tried to give them to Babs instead of to Lady McG., she being the prettiest person there.) . . .

ROCKHAMPTON — S.S. LUCINDA

Friday
June 10

Packed. Went to Carnival . . . An old man fell on my hat, and we saw the sideshows—a man "eating snakes" . . . he put them in his mouth— . . . On to the *Lucinda*—very exciting. We sleep in the saloon, B. and I. It is just curtained off. Evening: Going down the Fitzroy, crescent moon and comet and phosphorus . . . (**Lady McGregor comes and shoos Capt. Scarlett away whenever he talks to me—so funny**.)

ST. BEES

Saturday
June 11

Got up, making silly jokes to each other. We had not slept much and our heads ached . . . Arrived at a beautiful strait between two islands—Keswick and St. Bees. Landed on the latter—mountains and sandy beach, paddled ashore and gathered shells and the *most* delicious oysters. Capt. Scarlett walked on them without knowing what they were—he never saw them growing that way. He tried to cut his like an apple . . .

Sunday
June 12

Nice and hot, but I had a bad headache, so did not enjoy things as much as I should otherwise have done. We passed beautiful little islands and splendid coastline, but did not stop anywhere. Getting to know Babs better. **She is thorny but charming in many ways.** Passed through Whitsunday Passage, which is beautiful . . .

YARRABAH

Monday
June 13

Got up just in time to see Hinchinbrook passage. Even more beautiful than Whitsunday Passage—rather like a tropical edition of one of the Sounds—and the sea was like a smooth blue-and-silver opal. The big mountains had bright silver clouds on them—like Jupiter's. We didn't stop at Russell I., as we had meant to and gather oysters, for a strong wind came up. We went straight on to Yarrabah and anchored behind Fitzroy Island where the incorrigibles . . . are sent, feeling awfully disappointed and rather sick, and it rained like mad so we ate anchovy sandwiches.

Tuesday June 14

The wind freshened and we raced up to Cooktown and played at feeling ill and really enjoyed ourselves very much. Will be so sorry to put up our hair again. We wrote letters and read. Nothing much happened.

COOKTOWN   *Wednesday June 15*

Cooktown is a pretty little place, very tropical and quite dead. It rained rather. We got there on Tuesday night, but only landed for a stroll, and next day they drove us up with grey horses to a "wine" party, and to hospitals and schools (*how* we wanted to go rowing up the Endeavour as Captain Craig suggested) and saw views and so on. The views were really charming, and I never saw such a lot of blackfellows before. We opened the show, a very one-horse (and horsey) affair—lots of wild girls riding—and had a stiff queer lunch in a tent, and a really nice tea with the ladies, and went and opened the Agricultural half of the show at night. The fruit was really marvellous. Granadillas—five corners, pawpaws, all very fine. We were fairly tired—

Went out four miles to see a beautiful garden. It belongs to a funny old Jew who is very kind. Dan Solomon . . . We ate granadillas and drank milk under a jackfruit tree, and saw custard-apples for the first time, on their own trees . . . In the evening we went to a Musical Competition. So funny. Seven children in turn recited a ghastly thing called *Becalmed*—ga-ga . . .

Thursday June 16

COOKTOWN — PORT DOUGLAS

Left Cooktown at 8 a.m. and fought down to Port Douglas against a strong headwind. Babs and I felt horribly ill (and weren't) and *could* not get up till the ship was in at 12 and then it was a beastly rush and we had no breffus or lunch and went to a tea on a tumbler of champagne, and then on a sugar-

Friday June 17

train up to Mossman. Port Douglas is very pretty and the scenery along the track is all fine, but it certainly was rather wet. Went all over the Mossman mill and saw the crushing—*fascinating*, and inspected a school and examined the children and trammed for miles and miles . . . and had a fearfully long wine party and came home after 12—dead.

PORT DOUGLAS — CAIRNS

Saturday
June 18

Dead! and we were off by 9, tramming again through lovely scenery—mountains and forests and cane-fields—and we rode on the engine, and Captain S. gave us cigarettes, and I'll never forget how lovely that was. Schools again, and a 3 mile beach hard as blue metal, and home by 1. Chewed the sugar-cane a nice man sent us . . . and then flopped absolutely, dead with sleep. Cairns is pretty. There has been a row with the Mayor and things are mad. Addresses and a mile-long concert (Caledonian). *Bed.*

CAIRNS — CHILLAGOE

Monday
June 20

Left Cairns by the railway that passes the Barron Falls . . . Reached Chillagoe to find a different climate, dry and wonderfully clear. Stayed with the mine-manager, who has a fascinating tropical house and a nice tall blue-eyed wife. A scrumptious dinner and then we drove to the Caves—bright moon. We had a splendid scramble through them. Supper (such a good one) was set in a huge cave, and we scrambled on with a nice thin man called Campbell, who took us (just B. and me, the others had given out) to a cave no women had been to: and we were so proud.

CHILLAGOE — ATHERTON

Tuesday
June 21

Went over the works, after hearing Mrs Horsburgh whistle, which she does wonderfully. Left for Atherton, and passed out of that clear hot weather very regretfully. It was raining at Atherton and the red mud was even thicker than the roses, which is saying a lot. We were never so bunched before. Banquet and bed—in fearfully damp sheets. We had to sleep in our coats.

ATHERTON — CAIRNS

Wednesday
June 22

Went to school, Exhibition Hospital, Foundation stone laying (interesting) and show and lunch, pouring rain most of the time. Rush for train, weather changing quickly as we left . . . Cairns at 8. People to dinner, during which I felt queer, and towards the end I was taken upstairs where I fainted comfortably. Done up, I suppose. Humiliating —

CAIRNS — GERALDTON — MOURILYAN

Thursday
June 23

Came to Geraldton, a pretty place, but it was too rough to land, so we went on to Mourilyan, an exquisite little harbour with an entrance only 75' wide. Lovely hills and jungle. We stayed on board, and I finished *An Amazing Marriage*, for we didn't feel inclined to write letters . . .

MOURILYAN — RATTLESNAKE ISLAND — TOWNSVILLE

Saturday
June 25

Reached Rattlesnake I. fairly early. There are lovely shells there, we three nearly went mad with joy, and we paddled and ate lots of oysters, and built sandcastles. We left after hours, to our sorrow, and slept till Townsville. Afternoon: Reception and long circus procession, and nice tea and sunset, and splendid mail awaiting us . . .

Sunday   June 26   TOWNSVILLE — TRAIN

Church, Presbyterian. I was awfully shocked. They announced the Governor and everybody stood up—as if it were a drawing room . . . After lunch we went to a huge hospital, an orphanage (ugh!) and a Bishop . . . After dinner we went in the train and it was bitterly cold (a beautiful train), and we couldn't turn out the electric light so we turned pauv' P'tit Chose* out of his peaceful bed.
n.b. He looks so nice in bed.

P'tit Chose: Dorothea's pet name for, possibly, G. L. Byth, Private Secretary to Sir William MacGregor.

CHARTERS TOWERS — TOWNSVILLE

Wednesday   June 29

Went down the Brilliant Extended goldmine—3,000 ft. vertically—very dirty but *awfully* interesting: the cage you go down in, the queer trolley rattling down at an angle of 38 degrees—the naked men (well, half-naked—) and the stifling passages where it isn't ventilated, and the gold brick at the top, and the quicksilver squeezed through a cloth—o-oh—I *loved* it all. Then we went to a hospital, dirty as we were, and all the patients were cheerful and told me their life histories . . .

TOWNSVILLE — S.S. LUCINDA

Captain Scarlett stole a holiday for us. It was a glorious day—and so B. and I went with Captain Craig and another sailorman to Magnetic Island instead of to meatworks and foundation stones. We steered the launch and paddled and had lunch at the nice hotel where the old man was much intrigued, and looked at the coral, and came home to write letters with a pleasant sense of guilt . . .

*Thursday
June 30*

ABBOT BAY — BOWEN

Read letters from Mother and Ruth. Babs gave me a lovely lace handkerchief. Landed at Abbot Bay, a beautiful place, with a river and swarms of stingarees, and oysters of much succulence. Paddled and nearly got lost in quicksand and smoked and saw *bêche de mer*—loathsome stuff. Reached Bowen in the afternoon. Usual shivoo, and a very pleasant drive round fruit farm (mangosteens, pomeloes and candlenuts—and some soursop). Evening: *Conversazione.* Mr Alexander Mackenzie, very *toqué* stood firmly on my dress—tried to hold my hand while he said what a darling Babs was.

*Friday
July 1*

Sir William opened the Bowen-Proserpine Railway, and they let us ride on the engine. The engineer, Timmy Macrae, was a white-toothed Dear, and so

*Saturday
July 2*

was his brother Jack, the stoker. He let us *drive*! We each drove 23 miles and it was heavenly. We *were* happy. Proserpine is a sugar place. Banquets and mills — very nice but tiring . . .

BRAMPTON ISLAND

Monday July 4

. . . Got to a nice island where a big turtle was slowly swimming ashore. Heaps of *bêche de mer* . . . I waded ashore in my folly because Hug-You-Gug-Hug* taunted me. (That guard's language is curiously alluring. One finds oneself practising it at all sorts of times.) . . .

MACKAY

Tuesday July 5

I don't think I like Mackay. It was hot and muggy. Beautiful thick groves of coco palms—but the Programme was so *very* long and one had to go through it all. Train journey to the Marian sugar mill (house where Melba used to live, when her husband beat her an' all) . . .

PORT CLINTON

Thursday July 7

Stayed in bed for breakfast—felt awfully weak and headachey. Got up and teased Petit Chose, who gave us oysters. Port Clinton is most beautiful, but I felt too limp to land. The others did.

There are mountains and mountains and mountains all round it.

BUNDABERG — TRAIN

Friday July 8

Packed and felt doleful at leaving *Lucinda* . . . Train, very cold, but slept well on the whole.

TRAIN — GOVT. HOUSE BRISBANE (FERNBERG)

Saturday July 9

Arrived grey dawn. Magnificent view from Fernberg (dawn lighting fires in the windows of the houses on the hill opposite). *Baths* and no rest. Too excited.

Hug-You-Gug-Hug: Hugh Scarlett's first name in his "private" language.

Seventeen letters, an awfully nice one from Ruth about H.H.C. Explored new house and loved B.'s tower room . . . Evening: Played billiards very badly, but very happily. Captain Scarlett and I were beaten hollow.

Opening of Parliament. Sir W. very gorgeous.* It didn't last long. In the afternoon we lay down. We all have sore throats and they make us feel feverish and tired . . .

In the evening Petit Chose and I went to the Assembly Ball . . . swarms of partners, excellent floor and cigarettes. Home an hour later than we said, flying in an open motor . . . I was excited and not in the least tired, had had a lovely time, and went to bed chuckling . . . Oh it was a purple evening! **I like him alone**. He is awfully frank then.

On July 21 Dorothea left Government House to stay with Robin Dods and his American-born wife Mary. Robert "Robin" Smith Dods (1868–1920) was a distinguished architect, much of whose work reflected a radical approach to design, particularly in the context of the Australian climate. He had undertaken work for the Bank of New South Wales, of which Charles Mackellar was president, and the two families had become friends. Robin and Mary Dods had two children: Lorimer, who later became an eminent doctor, and Elisabeth.

In writing about Robin Dods, Dorothea refers to him first as "Mr Dods" and "R.S.D.". As a clandestine relationship develops, he becomes "Robin" or "R.", invariably in code. To further conceal her feelings for Robin Dods, she sometimes follows a coded section with a longhand entry in which he is referred to as "Mr Dods". Where confusion may arise between Ruth and Robin, both of whom Dorothea calls "R.", I have replaced "R." with "Robin".

gorgeous: "Sir William McGregor [*sic*] wore his handsome Windsor uniform, over which was thrown a magnificent silk cloak, lined with crimson, the insignia of the G.C.M.G. On his breast glittered the star of the same order . . . In consequence of the Royal period of mourning many of the gowns were in black . . . Miss McGregor was also becomingly gowned in black with a picture hat, richly plumed, and a handsome set of chinchilla furs. Miss Mackellar (Sydney) . . . wore a smart coat and skirt of black cloth with a Napoleon hat, and a white feather stole." (*Brisbane Courier*)

[ABBOTT STREET] I love waking here. The room and the whole house is so beautiful . . .

Sunday
July 24

. . . Cold very bad and aching. Mrs Dods thought it better that I should not go to tennis at the Hudsons. I would only have been a dull ass. I sat in the sun with my hair down and wrote to Mother instead. In the evening they petted and doctored me and we went to bed fairly early. They *are* such dears!

Saturday
July 30

Still felt like influenza . . . Dined with Dr and Mrs Espie Dods. She's pretty and has a lovely voice (but does not sing well). Miss Stodart of the magnificent red hair was there, too. She made all the rest of us look white and weak.

Monday
August 1

Rather better. (I cough at night, and it keeps 'em awake—awkward!) . . . Evening: Tired and "placable", as R.S.D. [Robin Dods] said. Smoked peacefully and felt that everybody was nice. **Mrs D. went to bed early and he kept me up awfully late yarning. He's such a dear. It makes things really hard.**

Thursday
August 4

Strenuous work and cleaning of silver. Nice, but quite hard . . . Afternoon: Lay down and began to write, and Mr Dods came home and came *in* and began to yarn . . . and I was tired, but too silly to stop. Evening: It was a nice party, about 40 people came and everybody loved it, and Mrs Dods had an adorable pink brocade dress. She was a picture. I wore the brown and gold . . .

Saturday
August 6

   Nothing will ever stop me being a little fool.

The John Forrests' garden party for the Chelmsfords. Very nice. Talked to Babs and Captain Gaunt and Lord Chelmsford, who is a dear and pretended he knew me—and crowds of other people. Felt depressed and cranky. Evening: Mater Misericordiae Ball.* Went late and did not stay long—daunting floor, awfully funny to dance on . . . **He does like me, but he was very good driving home and I tried to help him and we succeeded! It will be all right now I think.**

Tuesday
August 9

Ball: Robin Dods was the architect of the new Mater Misericordiae Hospital. The ball was "an unqualified success in every way. Between 300 and 400 dancers occupied the floor. The hall was elaborately decorated with various shades of art muslin, flags, palms and other greenery. The large platform was festooned with pale blue muslin, and branches of peach blossom and bamboo were also introduced. The pillars round the ball room were completely hidden from view by greenery, in which was mingled pink roses and wattle blossom." (*Brisbane Courier*)

Thursday
August 18

Up for 8 o'c. breakfast. Horribly tired . . . Lunch at Bishopsbourne with two Bishops (one Arch), an archdeacon and two ordinary clergymen . . . The *Southern Sphere* arrived with that yarn "The Lie" *and* "The Coorong Sandhills". Evening: Dinner at the Bigge's. Nice. Mrs Bigge is a cat—it isn't her fault, but she is. Collapsed coming home—teeth chattering an' all. Ah bah—I hate my weakness.

Tuesday August 23

Went into town and lunched with Mr Dods in the gardens. **He *is* just a boy! It was nice! It lasted two hours though.** Went to the Terrace and picked up Babs and Betty. Motored to Govt. House with them, had tea and played round and then went to One Tree Hill. Elisabeth was so happy! It was a lovely day and the sunset was exquisite. Then back to Fernberg and home, both tired. Mrs Dods had a headache and went to bed, and we talked—and argued— and I told stories when the conversation got personal. He is easy to divert.

Thursday
August 25

. . . Wrote letters, paid calls and shopped, missed R.S.D. by five minutes. Awfully tired, but the calls were successful. Evening: . . . Mrs Dods was tired and nervous, and I wanted to go to bed and was too tired to say so—and **I think it is just as well that I'm going away, dear as they are** . . .

Dorothea's destination was Cressbrook on the Brisbane River, home of the McConnel family. For a week she explored the river, rode astride, admired the slab house built in 1841 and modernised by Robin Dods, and reported in code that it was dull and that she had smoked a reefer because there were no cigarettes.

CRESSBROOK — FERNBERG

Saturday
September 3

. . . Horrid train journey, long and hot . . . Nice to see Babs again, and Sir William too . . . Bed early. Babs came up and yarned and yarned and yarned till all was blue, the darling—I think she's glad I'm back.

Wednesday
September 7

. . . Rushed off after lunch to see the Siberian dogs and ponies that are going on the Scott Polar Expedition. Ponies (white) fearfully depressed, dogs hardly less so. Nice blue-eyed man called Bruce showed them to me. You say Chai

chai chai to go to the left and Tin tin tin for right, and Ta ta ta ta for go on . . . Patted *some* of them . . .

GOVT. HOUSE — ABBOTT STREET

Hot. Nerves, and felt really ill. Packed . . . R.S.D. called for me, and it was good, and I felt worn out, but bucked up during the evening. **Mrs D. has nerves, but I of all people and to her of all people ought to be patient.**

*Saturday
September 10*

. . . Called on lots of people (**nerves still**) . . . Evening: Mr Cookson, young Englishman, came. Nice thing, 600,000 acres in W.A. and an interest in everything, especially Ostriches and Sisalhemp. Mr Dods tried to give me a lovely old Italian pendant, but I wanted it too much. *Ahime*! I wish oneself would *let* oneself do these things—no, perhaps I don't really.

*Monday
September 12*

. . . **Nerves still—I am being good! Nobody helps me—oh what a baby I am!** . . .

*Tuesday
September 13*

After "rather choky goodbyes" Dorothea left Abbott Street on September 16. En route to Sydney she stayed at Gabbinbar, home of Lady Janet Nelson, widow of the late Queensland Premier and pastoralist Sir Hugh Nelson.

TRAIN — LIVERPOOL ST.

Smoked last cigarette. Read, and felt the journey very long. Mother and Father, the *darlings*, both came to meet me . . .

*Monday
September 19*

Large fat post, mainly from Queensland, including note from R.S.D. to say that he would arrive by the *Osterly* that morning. Tailor & general scramble. Called at the Australia and after some delay saw the aforesaid R.S.D. Afternoon: **Chiropodist**. Did me good.

*Monday
September 26*

63

Wednesday *September 28*	R.S.D. wants me to go to be examined because there may be something wrong with my heart, but I hate to, for various reasons . . .

Two days later Ruth visited Dorothea, bringing with her the first sketches for the novel on which they were to collaborate, The Little Blue Devil. *The hero of* The Little Blue Devil *is based on Tony—or, to give him his right name, Antony St Croix—one of their favourite play-characters. Antony St Croix is abandoned by his French father, at a tender age. The little black-eyed lad sets off to see the world and, as the years slip by, his reckless nature leads him into endless trouble. After many adventures, saved usually in the nick of time by a lovely lady, Tony descends into a pit of despair and degradation. Then he learns he is the rightful heir to a fortune and a title, both of which have passed to his cousin, a beautiful and pure English girl. Being at heart a gallant gentleman, Tony decides not to upset her by claiming his birthright. He chooses instead to fake his own death. There are more adventures, including a trek across a desert in Australia. Coincidences abound, and Tony's long journey finally ends in his cousin's arms.*

It is not recorded whether Dorothea was to wait until Ruth had proceeded further, or whether the unfortunate events of the next day distracted Dorothea from writing. Whatever the reason, it was not until Christmas Day of that year that she began work on The Little Blue Devil.

Saturday *October 1*	. . . Went to races feeling horribly ill and with a bad headache. Hated everybody, except R.S.D. And coming home, Boyle [the Mackellars' chauffeur] (not his fault) slammed the motor door on my hand. It was hard work to sit up and make conversation all the way home. Then I fainted, and the rest was bed and agony. They thought the bone was smashed, but it just escaped. Dad, the darling, read *The Descent of Man* to me, and gave me a sleeping draught.
Sunday *October 2*	Got up late, very sick and shaky. Hand giving me fits. R.S.D. came in the afternoon, but refused to go motoring because I couldn't. Lots of visitors came and I talked to them, and it was all like an evil dream. **He *is* nice to me!**
Monday *October 3*	Hand better, cold worse . . . Hopeless to think of going to the dance tonight . . . I

OPPOSITE: *Flowerpiece* Roy de Maistre

can't go to Dr Skirving* now, and it's on my nerves, and I feel rather a little wreck.

Tuesday
October 4

Stayed in bed and read, and nursed up my cold . . . Evening: Got up and went to the Australian Club Ball. I have never felt worse. I left at 11, for I could hardly stand—or speak. My voice had gone and my chest hurt like knives. **R. took me home. We drove in the park first—but indeed we were good about it and we're going to be so sensible.**
I don't know how I feel . . .

Wednesday
October 5

Mother got the Doctor worry out of me . . . Doctor Skirving came in the afternoon and poked me and said I was altogether run-down, but not organically wrong, and I needed more clay, and R.S.D. came, very worried, and we all talked. He came to my room and said the bed should be moved, so he and Mac moved it and I felt limp and fairly calm. Evening: Just reading. Read books of sonnets that he brought and *The Story of the Guides* (Younghusband) and *A Corner of Spain* and Wilde's *Ideal Husband.*

Thursday
October 6

Bed. Less pain in chest . . .**R.S.D. and I was very weak and I gave in without saying anything—but he knows I like him now and I'm glad in a queer way.** It is only a little, but I never did before—and it shakes me dreadfully. He stayed to dinner, and the family all sat in my room and talked—it was so nice.

Friday
October 7

Dr Skirving came and said I was better (which was true), but would not let me get up, and Babs—and R.S.D.—arrived. She looked so sweet. After lunch she and Mother went out for a drive and Bertha came, and they stayed, and we had a good talk, and he went away to Queensland and **I miss him so** and Babs and I yarned. He has frightened her so that she will not let me exert myself at all—it's funny . . .

Saturday
October 8

. . . The Dudleys [Governor-General Lord Dudley and Lady Dudley] asked us both to go to the races, but I was not allowed. I went for a drive with M. and saw Isabel MacCallum, who was amusing and a dear, but I felt horribly

Skirving: Robert Scot-Skirving, eminent surgeon, diagnostician and a family friend.

66

nervous and shaky, as if people would make me scream. No dances—Lady Poore's was last night and Lady Gould tonight—*ahime*! . . .

Tuesday October 11

. . . Government House, to a concert-meeting thing . . . Heaps of well-dressed acquaintances. Felt absurdly and miserably shy, likewise tired . . .

Friday October 14

Voted [State election] . . . Typed a little (I can't use my middle finger yet) and wrote a letter or two. Evening: . . . Very nice and cheery . . . We talked elections a good deal. Everybody thinks there will be a Labour majority, and Mother is so wild! Well—she's right. It's awfully important.

Monday October 17

. . . read *Madame Margot*. Good—*very* outspoken—odd how one doesn't mind things when they're shoved a few centuries back and talked of in another language! . . .

Sunday October 23

Church at 11. Mr Pitt preached on the crisis at S. James.* I expect the Archbishop will make rows about it. Evening: Just plain evening . . .

The next day Dorothea went to stay with her brothers at Kurrumbede. On returning home on November 5 she found "a large bill and a small cheque—so characteristic of my financial affairs!".

. . . Bertha came in just before supper, very shy and sweet, to tell us she's engaged to Captain Prowse. Lucky man! . . .

Sunday November 6

. . . Tidied out old desk and threw away a lot of treasured rubbish. Rushed to lunch with Ruth. Acted Prevost play and a little of George's new girl, which

Friday November 11

James: The "crisis" concerned the appointment of a new rector at St James, King Street, a High Anglican church. The "low" Anglican Archbishop Wright required an undertaking from the new appointee that he would not wear "Popish" eucharistic vestments.

by the way, went extremely well. All this was sandwiched with talk. It was a disagreeable, blustering day, with a hot wind and rain . . .

Tuesday
November 15

. . . Got exciting Canadians* with stockings and handkerchiefs to match, and put them on for Dad's benefit. I think that in his heart he liked them . . .

Wednesday
November 16

. . . Father and Mother went out to dinner. Babs and I read and knitted and chose verses for "booklet"*—I hate that word, but it's true. We had such a good evening, and we skylarked too.

Thursday
November 17

Dr Bennet and a little shopping. He talked much more than he ought and **hinted scandalous things**—Sat with Babs (packing sadly) and knitted. Afternoon: She went . . . and I tried to arrange book a little . . .

Friday
November 18

First motor driving lesson in Centennial Park. Most successful. I drove her home. The gears are easier than in the Siddeley. *Lovely* ! I feel so happy. Afternoon: Met Will Masefield and some others at Australia and went to cricket. NSW v S. Africa. Very good, and we were a jolly party . . . Dinner here. Sir Normand, Sir S. Griffith* and Ladies and Mr Johnson. Rather dears. I was feeling quite fit and so proud of my family.

Saturday
November 19

. . . Mrs Alec Gordon's party for Gladys Owen. **Dorothy Owen there. She was a good deal more uncomfortable than I was, I think**—She looked so pretty. **I bowed to her but did not speak** — . . .

Monday
November 21

. . . Joined R. at Phillip St. Bathed at Rose Bay. Water nice and not very cold. Out to the Heads, acted ever so much. It was a lovely day. Did Prevost play, and George's girl and the Trents and the Islanders too, and thoroughly enjoyed our bread and butter. Home very late, finding Babs here. Both tired and sleepy. Arranged book a little. Bed dog-tired. But oh, the day was good!

Canadians: Two-piece swimwear consisting of long woolly knickers and a matching singlet reaching to mid-thigh.
booklet: Following Charles Bean's suggestion, Dorothea was compiling her first poetry anthology, *The Closed Door*. It comprised previously unpublished poems and those which had already appeared in the *Spectator*, *Harper's*, the *Bulletin*, the *Sunday Times, Bush Brother, Southern Sphere* and *Appleton's*.
Griffith: Sir Samuel Walker Griffith, Premier of Queensland 1883–88, and first Chief Justice of the High Court of Australia.

. . . Despatched *Closed Door** . . .

. . . A. Allen's* dinner at Paris House and Tivoli afterwards . . . Marvellous performing dogs (I hate that sort of thing really) and two wonderful and improper French dancers. The woman fascinated me—great play of expression.

. . . Heard that Florence had broken two ribs, but when we went to see her she was gone. Scribbled play-things. Evening: Read Mary Coleridge (delightful) and laughed and tickled M.'s foot.

. . . **Pining to act**! . . .

Friday December 2

. . . Ruth came for a little while and I acted Lalage,* lying on the sofa. It was a relief . . .

Tuesday December 6

Shopping, went to Station to meet Mrs Dods and the children. Elisabeth was very glad to see me, the darling, and nearly kissed my veil off . . . Home. Mrs Dods and the children, whom I entertained playing with quicksilver . . . Miss Antonia Williams —a fearsome old bird—and her quite unexpected companion came to dinner. Abigail  Child, looked 32 till we asked her to go bathing, when she flushed and dimpled. She's only 22. She hasn't seen *anything*, ever, and she's starving for life. We're going to take her to the theatre, and so on. Poor child! Our lives are shot with scarlet and green and gold compared to hers.

Door: The Closed Door was despatched to H. H. Champion of the Australasian Authors' Agency. Some contribution towards the cost of printing was made by Dorothea in February 1911.
Allen's: Arthur Allen, senior partner of Allen, Allen & Hemsley, solicitors, an enthusiastic patron of the arts.
Lalage: a play-character.

Wednesday *December 7*	. . . Went to R.'s and acted Lalage for a little. Rushed home and dressed with a pitchfork for lunch at *Kirkton* . . . Evening: Waited for Father, knitting, but he was getting his Bill through (Nurses) and was very late . . .
Thursday *December 8*	Called for The Child [Abigail], tea at Civil Service Stores, then Hardy's where we tried on the £690 earrings . . .
Monday *December 12*	. . . By lunchtime it was a downpour, so we could not go bathing, and I asked The Child (she has asked me to call her Abigail and I'm glad to) to come and spend the afternoon. I finished knitting the comforter and we talked a lot. She told me many things of her sad little life—horribly tragic . . .
Tuesday *December 13*	. . . Storm. All of us very restless. Heaps of electricity. I let some off on the typewriter. Evening: Read. General conversation, and we were all very glad we *had* had some books before we died.
Friday *December 23*	. . . Bathed with R. She was disturbed because I 'fessed that I might be going away. So was I. We came home and acted Kid Prevost, which was a great relief. Evening: Father went away, the dear, loaded like a goods train . . .
Saturday *December 24*	. . . Motored about with M. and Mrs. Brady, calling and leaving presents. Called on . . . Florence, who has broken her ribs again. Long afternoon. Nice post came at 20 to 7 with more presents, I was childishly excited . . . Early bed. I wake so horribly early nowadays.

Church. Wrote letters in a kimono—so did Mother. We got through such a lot. I was purring because of the Florentine pendant—After lunch there was time to do a little of *The Little Blue Devil.* I began at the beginning and was

surprised to find even that stiff part easy . . . Afterwards we went to the Bradys. I was very tired and in a silly mood. I won the Kim game and talked nonsense . . .

Thursday December 29

. . . Lay down and did not go out at all. Babs went away. Felt very ill.

Sunday January 1 1911

. . . Wrote letters and felt floppy. A bad beginning!

... Sat under the banyah tree and stared at the harbour ...

Sunday
January 1   1911

... I was told that Mr Newmarch was at the telephone. A very young voice said that it [Mr Newmarch] was a friend of Jim Fairfax and could it come to see me—could it come now because it had the horrors? Am I a friend? Of course it could. It did. It writes plays and very good verse, a bit of a genius I think—Father talked to it nearly all the time. 25 years old.

Monday
January 2

... The genius came and I took him in hand and—oh my soul and body! **He wants to marry me.** He has promised not to speak of it again. **He told me all his affairs, which are tangled, and his woes, which are tragically boyish**—and he's very young, and egotistical and sensitive and he will be hard to keep in hand. Jealous and frightfully highstrung. Poor child.

Tuesday
January 3

Two days later Dorothea left Sydney to visit Mrs Dods, who had retreated from the heat of Queensland's summer to Leura in the Blue Mountains, and her friend Meg McPhillamy at Bathurst. She worked on The Little Blue Devil—*"just a few pages every day, but it all helps"—and returned home on February 1.*

... Bathe. Not very nice. The sides full of minute brown worms. I discovered them as I got out, and spent some time getting them off me and trying not to be hysterical. Evening: Went to Lyons Terrace and looked at wedding presents and Bertha's trousseau ... Interesting talk from Father about capital and dividends.

Friday
February 3

Dentist (pretty bad) ... Home to rest ... and translate some more *coplas** [verses] ...

Tuesday
February 7

> *My love is like the telephone*
> *Upon a stormy day. I call*
> *And call, and call, and call in vain,*
> *For Central answers not at all.*

---

coplas: In November 1910 Dorothea had begun taking Spanish lessons. A Madrid newspaper ran a competition for *coplas modernas* (modern verses). It subsequently printed over 600 verses, many of which Dorothea translated.

Evening: The Child [Mr Newmarch] came. **He's easier to manage when we are face to face than at a distance**! But I see breakers ahead . . .

LIVERPOOL ST. — MITTAGONG

Left at 8.30 for Mittagong in a motor with Dad and Mr George Beeby (the new Labour Minister for Education) and his wife. Nice journey up—dreaming of Tony and Lalage and verses. Inspection of Homes. Very interesting. Nice matrons . . . *Such* a full day! It was satisfactory too, specially for Dad. Mr Beeby is not half bad.

Sunday February 12

MITTAGONG — LIVERPOOL ST.

. . . Pouring rain, roads very bad . . . The chauffeur, a large and masterful person who addressed me as Mrs Doctor Mackellar, or for short—Mrs Doctor, insisted on covering me up, though none of us told him he could. I rather liked him . . .

Monday February 13

. . . Added a few paragraphs to R.'s chapters of *L.B.D.* . . . Evening: The Child rang up and asked me to go to Mosman with him. Indeed he is quite mad . . .

Tuesday February 14

. . . Bertha sent for me to say Goodbye, which was a choky affair, though we did our best to be commonplace. Then took Elisabeth and Florence to the railway station and got them into a sleeper with their luggage. I couldn't have believed that Florence would get so fussed. Awfully tired and teeth aching all day. Evening: Talk with the family about Mother before she was married— the dear!

Wednesday February 15

. . . Bertha's wedding.* Horribly huge, and I never saw so many big hats and bad behaviour . . . Dressed her—bless her! and she looked sweetest undressed . . .

Thursday February 16

Rainy day. Servants all ill. Made bed . . .

Sunday February 19

wedding: Bertha Brady and Captain Prowse were married at St Andrew's Cathedral. "The bride . . . wore a lovely gown of soft white satin and chiffon, a square train detached. The bodice was trimmed with Limerick lace and hand-embroidered with pearls. She wore a little cap of Limerick lace beneath her tulle veil and carried a sheaf of lilies of the valley." (*Sydney Morning Herald*)

OPPOSITE: *The Selection* Julian Ashton

Tuesday *February 21*	. . . Darned stockings (King [Dorothea's maid] still in bed) . . . Wrote a few pages of *L.B.D.* . . .
Friday *February 24*	. . . Miss Potter's (very goodlooking young suffragette) reception at the Australia, a queer collection. Met an insane female Bulletinist, Miss Dickinson, and Miss Rose Scott.* Came back to Grace Palotta. V. sweet and amusing, but I had to rush away and help Father get M.'s birthday present. ("I donno what to get y'r Mother!") . . .
Saturday *February 25*	. . . Mother was pleased with the "tippits", as Father will call the *jabots*. Made verses about a witch and a dead man.
Wednesday *March 1*	Bathed, washed hair, and afterwards did an awfully long and exciting scene with Tony and Glynde and it made us very late; so we went and had lunch in town instead of going home. I love being wicked that way—so good for the temper! . . .
Friday *March 3*	. . . Acted a lot—Tony and the Tempest-Hollands (and they've fallen in love, bless their hearts!) . . . Home quite late. Lots of telephoning and trying on of blouses for Mother, and a few play-letters, but there was not time for many. So-o sleepy.
Monday *March 6*	Diamond Bay. A perfect day, all blue and gold. We acted ever so much and I was almost too happy to breathe. Ruth was a dear, and there were charming lizards and goats about (one who played at being petrified) and we were wicked and stayed very late. I'm 'fraid I tired her, poor darling, but she did like it too, and it was all most satisfactory. We began two new plays and did lots of pleasing things . . .

On March 8 Dorothea and her mother set off in their chauffeur-driven car for Kurrumbede. Dorothea reports that she had driven "a good way" when

---

Rose Scott: Campaigner for women's rights. In 1904 she had worked closely with Charles Mackellar on the preparation of his *Infant Protection Act*, which secured the rights of an unmarried mother to sue the father of her child for support and maintenance.

the car foundered in deep water at a crossing. The car was rescued by "various Samaritans" but had broken a cylinder. Leaving Boyle, the chauffeur, to mend the car, Dorothea and her mother spent next day "reading sixpenny books" at West Maitland before taking the evening train to Gunnedah.

[KURRUMBEDE] After the usual sort of journey we arrived . . . and it was all heavenly—and the garden a dream. Never have I seen such grass as in the paddocks . . .

Lazed, Read *Lifes* . . . Drove down to the river to see the bullocks taking timber across. 28 of them. A good sight . . . Evening: . . . Tidied papers—or tried to.

Beautiful day, but I felt "crook". Wrote a good deal, including some letters. Tony is in London now, and it is not specially easy to do—easier when the disclosure comes, I expect! Dad went away, and before he went he suddenly said I must not ride Silver. No time to argue, but it made me angry, and depressed me so much that I really can't write any more about Monday!

Wrote some *L.B.D.* (only a little) . . . Walked down to the river, very grass-seedy. Took 'em nearly all out of my stockings and walked home barefoot. Met Mac and went out for a drive to take stores to Jack Dean. Lovely day and the stumps were all hidden, so we had a gloriously exciting time! The Deans' child (18 months old) drinks tea and is as yellow as a guinea, poor babe . . .

Wrote *L.B.D.* . . . wrote verses about the Sunset Rainbow. Looked at the splendid moon—with the telescope.

. . . After church went riding with Eric and took a stubborn lot of sheep from Redbank to Culgai . . . and saw black duck and swans and got back in time for tea.

Got up early and gathered armfuls of roses, for the rain in the night had brought them out . . . Afterwards went out mustering with Eric to Emu and Vicky Castle. Came home after sunset. None in the west, but the eastern sky all pink clouds, the rest pink and gold swirls on a bright blue background . . .

Packed. Felt miserable. Both the dear boys came in. Eric drove Mother with Tan and Tony and I went with Mac and the Virginian. The shortest drive I ever had. I do hate leaving them—and Kurrumbede . . . Long wakeful night.

Thursday
March 23

Got home very punctually, unpacked and began copying out verses at once . . . **Felt ill.** Lots of telephoning to answer, including The Child.

Friday
March 24

Lay and read *Ailsa Paige* and thought of ideas for plays . . . Norman Pilcher came to supper . . . **I don't know if we are getting into deep water or not, but I rather suspect it.** He stayed very late.

Sunday
March 26

. . . R. came and we had a short but very successful spurt of acting the Remington* play. I have been either Remington or Rags ever since—the former very angry and troubled, the latter in a passion of fear and shame. Most uncomfortable! Afternoon: Lots of shopping, got 2 nice hats. One, a *darling*—black straw with yellowy brown roses . . . Evening: Wrote *L.B.D.* Slept badly. Remington!

Monday
March 27

. . . Went to R. and acted out Remington, which went well. Thank *goodness*, we're not falling in love yet. I'm so tired of that . . . Then we walked across the park together to my meeting (the Tottie cough-drop hat is a great success) and I stayed there *two hours* forming a constitution for The Applied Arts Depot Club and arguing as to the virtues of men with Miss Rose Scott . . .

Tuesday
March 28

. . . I'm getting hard-up again and the expenditure has been so *dull*, too!

Wednesday
March 29

Ô jour funeste! Four meetings—and the Archbishop ran me into begging at doors—and Lord Chelmsford—Oh, I hate meetings—and by the evening I was a rag. At eight o'clock we had to go and work for the girls' dance, and I addressed envelopes until my arm nearly dropped off, feeling old and haggard among all those young things . . .

Tuesday
April 4

Still tired, one night is not enough to rest in after a day like that! . . . Dad

Wednesday
April 5

Remington: A play-character, later the subject of *Two's Company*, a novel co-written with Ruth Bedford.

OPPOSITE: *Moonrise, Heidelberg* E. Phillips Fox

told me that a boy at the Grammar School published "Core of my Heart" ["My Country"] as his the other day. Funny! . . .

Saturday April 8

The Book [The Closed Door] arrived! I never dreamed it would be so soon. Mother and I awfully excited and so was Ruth when she came . . . Went to Seaward and saw motor boat race with Tony Hordern's new Hydro plane that won the World Championship at Monaco last year. It's—it's quite superhuman. I *loved* watching it—like a comet or a swordfish . . .

Sunday April 9

. . . All sorts of rhymes stirring in my head, but none came. I wish I didn't get so tired.

Tuesday April 18

. . . At 6.30 felt tired and depressed, but it went off. The Govt. House Shivoo (Cranbrook) was like most of 'em, but at least I saw a lot of people that I wanted to, and on the whole I enjoyed it. Selfish way of talking! But the others didn't much.

Wednesday April 19

Tailor. Blue tailormade. A great success . . . Wrote a rhyme that rather pleased me. I think I'll call the next book Apes and Peacocks.* Evening: Girls' Dance. I like the responsibility of being hostess . . . **but I'm a little afraid of Norman Pilcher! He would be so hard to stop if he once began to make love**—and I do like him.

Saturday April 22

Bed all day. Ruth came, the Samaritan, and scolded me, but she was a great comfort, and I read her *L.B.D.* which is convincing . . . Oh yes, and *The Bulletin* wants my photograph to publish, please—How queer! Dad says I must because it doesn't do to offend them —

Peacocks: A recurring theme in Dorothea's writings was the idea that her world was peopled by effortlessly elegant and successful "peacocks" and by "apes" who failed with their vulgar imitations.

... Talked first to Malcolm then to Mother then to Dad, so could not go out, but that is Duty—and I love it. Dad lectured me about being thin. "Yo'r face is—ridiculous."* ...

No church. Cold very bad ... **Diarrhoea** (how d'you spell it?) too. I've never been more of a wreck. Evening: Mr Lark and Mr Pilcher and **as I took him to the lift, he sprung a gold cigarette holder and a proposal on me**— Oh *dear*. And he had to come back and talk aviation for three solid hours —

The next day Dorothea left Sydney to stay with Babs MacGregor at Government House in Brisbane, even though her father did not think she was well enough to travel. "It was like a happy dream to see Babs and Meg at the station."

[FERNBERG] Wrote heaps of letters and three pages of Tony. Afternoon: Governor-General came to lunch with Captain Rowe (nice talk about prize fighting) and the G.G. crawled about on the veranda and taught us knots. Afterwards we sewed in the tower, and read Dubarrolles. Evening: Mandolins in the tower.

... Glorious day. Felt sick—all of us. Went outside the Heads and fished and forgot everything. I broke the record, getting 22 within an hour, to my joy and the Scots bo'sun's ... Then we landed and the sea was absolutely chrysoprase, and the beach wonderful. Oh, it *hurt* with beauty! Then up the river with the lights *dolce melancolia*—is that right?—and bed very early. Encouraging letter from H.H.C., who says I sell fifth in Australia.

... Got nice *Daily Telegraph* notice of book. Races. Very nice, only I didn't bet. Saw nearly everybody in Brisbane except those I love best. Evening: Pretty tired and rather hysterical.

ridiculous: This was an era when plumpness was the ideal—and attainable by all, according to the Falliere Flesh-Food Company. "Thin, run-down, flat-chested women—cover your scraggly shoulders with subterfuge and hide your lack of figure with pads as much as you like during the daytime—the night will find you out. It is when evening dress becomes a necessity that your lack of development gives you the greatest worry ... There is no denying that the real charm and first impression a woman gives are created by the possession of a good figure. A full, well-rounded bust glorifies a woman much more than a pretty face ... By following our advice thousands of women who had for years endured the mortification of a chest devoid of even a suggestion of bust development are now possessed of fully-developed, well-rounded figures, full, firm well-rounded cheeks, arms, neck and shoulders." (*Sydney Morning Herald*)

FERNBERG — ABBOTT ST.

Tuesday
May 30

. . . Mr Dods called for me, and driving home told me that Mrs Dods was without a cook and **nervous—so's he**—and so am I. All shivers. Hospital Ball. . . *Very* good. Danced with five Germans at once. **Walked up and down the street before going to bed.** Not a bit tired.

Wednesday
May 31

. . . Mr Gould came to dinner and we talked shop, and he and R.S.D. both want me to break with H.H.C., but I'm nervous about doing it, first because I don't want to hurt his feelings and secondly because I hate rows.

BRISBANE — CAMBOOYA

Thursday
June 1

. . . Inauguration of Queensland University. Impressive but very long. *Hundreds* of *ad eundem* degrees and long speeches. Professor Wilson's was excellent . . . **He isn't as trying as you might think. He's very good—for a man.**

Thursday
June 8

Housework. Nice. No writing though . . . Nice evening and I did bendings and dances wifout any stays. Now, was that Bold?

Friday
June 9

. . . **I love having my tea brought to me by him in the morning—he's rather a dear.** Mr Dods' birthday.

Saturday
June 24

. . . Went to town and shopped and saw **R. for half an hour, which was very good—(But not good of me.)** Afternoon: . . . The Mayoral Garden Party which was unexpected fun . . . We had tea under a big tent and everybody else looked hungrily at our piles of strawberries . . .

On June 26 Dorothea returned to Fernberg. A fortnight later she set off to visit a number of country friends.

Tuesday July 4

. . . Motored to Talgai, a station of Mr Ramsay's. Fascinating old place. It was very big once. Lunched there at a huge round mahogany table, slid dishes across . . . Glorious drive home. Evening: Poker Patience. Great fun. I am not so stupid at that as I expected.

Opposite: *The Flowershop* Thea Proctor

IPSWICH — NANANGO

Monday
July 10

. . . Jolly journey, but after Toogooloowah the scenery got beautiful. Arrived ankle deep in red dust . . . Not tired at all. Everything was so new . . . Miss Wigram met us with a lantern . . . she is a dear. A horse poked her head in at my window immediately and later drank the water in the basin . . .

NANANGO — CRESSBROOK

Wednesday
July 19

Got up 4.30 after restless night. Stars and moon. Very cold . . . Started with Alick in the dawn—glorious drive, for the day was fine, only the rain had made the road heavy—hard on the horses. Train journey long. Lovely welcome at Cressbrook—and *hot bath* . . .

Thursday
July 20

Nice lazy golden morning. Took lunch out to the river two miles down, and I read *The Silverado Squatters* aloud while the others worked, and then I bathed quite naked in the cool green water and rolled in the warm brown grass to dry myself. Evening: Danced bending dances. Lazed by fire while they went to Station Vale.

Friday
July 21

Went out riding (Billy—astride) with Barbara all down by the river and through the scrub, and back again on the other side . . . Evening: Message from the Dods asking me to stay for the Show, five or six dances, and three weeks—upsetting—and nice—and—Read Kipling to all and afterwards consulted with Beatrice and drifted into Limericks . . .

CRESSBROOK — NEW FARM

Monday
July 24

. . . Motored down to Brisbane—Barbara, Mrs David, Cissy and me. Lovely . . . Not a bit tired. Found that Mother had telegraphed that I could stay. (**Damn**!) Nice to be here.

Tuesday
July 25

Did not go to Babs, having no clothes. Wrote? in upper room. Shopped for stockings and things . . . Settling down a little, but still **angry and trapped** . . .

Wednesday
July 26

. . . **Teased R., which he deserves, though it was Mrs D. who asked me to stay! Would quarrel with him if he'd let me.** Went out calling with Mrs D. Evening: At home as usual, and just as nice as ever.

Awfully tired, and a queer pain in my side, over the breast. Couldn't go out . . . *Horrid* pain.

Was made to breakfast on the nursery veranda in the sun and a dressing gown. Washed hair. Wrote a letter or so. Did not go out at all.

. . . R. met me in Finneys and **would insist on buying me stockings.** Childish and funny, because we saw ever so many of our friends. Made me late for lunch, which I had alone. Went to see Babs. Fairly satisfactory, but I fear I'm rather on her nerves . . .

Friday August 4

. . . Fairly tired—poor Mrs Dods very much so. Evening: Talk. **(It's not easy, she's so nervous and I am growing to like him better. I can't help that.)**

Saturday August 5

Washed glasses and did odd jobs including burnt almonds. Afternoon: Arranged sweets and **R. talked to me, because there was nothing to do, but Mrs D. had nerves again**, being tired, poor dear, and **hated everything** . . .

Tuesday August 8

. . . Wrote a few letters and translated a little Dante . . . Assembly Ball. Mrs Dods didn't go. Very good. Only stayed 8 dances, but loved each one of them. **It will be some time before I forget the drive home, but it's too long to write here!** Only **he was touching me and—I said I was rather a bad little girl, and it hurt him. We were both upset and it got much more serious.** And I lost the carving Father gave me, which seemed to fit in—and I *was* so tired.

Got telegram from Eric saying Dindemah polo team beat Scone 9–1. Hurrah! Wired back.

The following day Dorothea felt ill and unsociable. The events of the previous evening had made a deep impression; she was almost at the point where she would admit she was in love. Soon she is acting with an uncharacteristic boldness—not altogether to Robin Dods' liking.

Thursday *August 10*	. . . R. was away and Mrs D. was ill! and Betty and I played together by the fire (the day was cold and wet) all day long. "Ships" and stories and Gibraltar— all manner of games. Lorimer arrived in the evening.
	After dinner we talked. **He was worried about me, and I told him something of what was in my heart, for indeed there has been a great change in the last two days.** A relief, but rather exhausting . . .
Friday *August 11*	Got up earlier than usual . . . Felt quite reasonably well. Evening: Mrs Arthur Feez's and Mrs W. Collins' dance. A very nice one, and I loved it—what I had of it. Broke down at the 12th dance. Rather a stirring night. **He was upset because I love him**, and it upset *me*, and **I nearly kissed him, which would have startled things** a good deal. I never felt like that before—rather desperate—and yet not miserable. Only he wouldn't believe me when I told him so.
Saturday *August 12*	. . . So tired, and that night things raced rather and suddenly ran down to a terrifying slackness—
Sunday *August 13*	. . . Lay on the river-bank smoking while the steamers went by . . . Evening: Good talk that ended not too well, but was patched up early—quite early. **The curse came evilly on in the night. Great pain.**
Monday *August 14*	**Stayed in bed with hot bottles and talked to Robin, which was strange and made me feel shy.** In the evening Mr Dods came home to his two invalids, and as Mrs Dods could eat nothing, he had dinner in my room, at her suggestion—and to the scandalization of Florence. Read heaps of poetry, heaps and *he-eaps.*

BRISBANE — TRAIN

Thursday *August 17*	**He came to me in the early morning and he said goodbye** . . . So hard to leave, and I felt ill—and the parlour car porter mothered me, and I read Bandello. It wasn't a bad sort of day. Train awfully crowded . . . Was grateful for the hampers, dreamed and slept.

. . . Lovely coming down through the Spring flowers. Mother at the station . . . So good to get home. The table covered inches deep with correspondence. My head whirled. Afternoon: Shopped. Ordered summer dresses and hats. Rather nice ones! . . .

Friday
August 18

. . . R. came, bringing the *L.B.D.* all typed and looking awfully nice. We talked spasmodically . . . and R. stayed to lunch. Afterwards we acted a little Remington, then tried the new engine of the car and went to Dunara,* where I gathered heaps of snowdrops from the bank. Evening: Margery came and we had a good yarn. She was very anxious to hear about Q., and I was surprised to find what lots of stories I couldn't tell.

Saturday
August 19

Monday   August 21

Mother not well—in bed. Anxious, restless time—and had to go out to post the *L.B.D.* and they made me send it as a parcel, and Dr Bennet kept me yarning ever so long, and Dr Thring* could not see me though I waited an hour—and I couldn't get the books I wanted for R.S.D. and I was so-o tired and worried . . . Dad came home and **I wanted Robin** and I want to tell everybody (nearly) about it . . .

Thursday   August 24

Wet. Dr Bennet. Dr Thring. Terrified. He *was* good to me. He advised me to ask Dad whether I could be examined under chloroform. I told Dad, who was a dear about it. He thinks (Dr. T.) that an operation will be necessary, but a very slight one . . . Evening: Wrote a letter or two. Feel much happier.

Sunday   August 27

. . . So dreadfully tired. N. Pilcher and The Child both rang up tonight. I said I was going away for a time—shunting things.

Dunara: The family home at Rose Bay, Dorothea's birthplace, leased in 1900 when the Mackellars moved to 183 Liverpool Street.
Thring: Edward Thring, leading gynaecologist.

Not enough time to go to the dentist, so decided to enjoy myself instead. Answered Bertram Stevens'* letter asking permission to include me in the *Golden Treasury* and another book—and gave "biographical details" as requested . . . Ruth. Talked a little and walked to the Domain . . . We discussed ways and means and finally decided to lunch there. We only had a shilling! We lunched successfully and had a lovely time. The hyacinths were splendid . . .

On August 30 Dorothea and her mother left Sydney for Kurrumbede, breaking the journey at Muswellbrook.

MUSWELLBROOK — KURRUMBEDE

Good day but roads pretty rough and soft after the rain. I drove from Scone to the Liverpool Ranges, but it tried poor M.'s nerves. She was continually fearing that I'd charge into cattle. Reached Gunnedah in the late afternoon and home at 5.45. Eric away shearing. Began unpacking and a slow luxurious reading of letters. (A very long one from Robin. I had not finished it by dinner time.) Eric came back and we talked, and after dinner he played some new things on the gramophone. "*What do you think of Hoolahan?*" etc. **I did so long to tell him about Robin—not names but just the fact**—

. . . So slack. I didn't even want to write or read . . . After lunch strolled to river. Lay on the green clover and thought of—nothing much. Went to The Shed with Mother, who was very sympathetic to the sheep and everybody, the darling. Felt ill and slacker still . . .

Less tired. Did flowers and wrote to Ruth and R. and read *Life* and *The Old Wives' Tale*. Malcolm arrived with Mr Dewhurst and Mr Turner . . . We all talked and played billiards . . . Then after tea we walked out and they had a few shots— poor little green parrots.

. . . "We" mustered the paddock and then Mac came. No, indeed it was not dull! . . . Went to shed and watched them drafting. Weighed myself (8 st. 8— not bad at all) . . .

Stevens: Bertram Stevens, publisher.

Tuesday *September 5*	. . . Watched the shearing. Made rhymes about swallows. Afternoon: Walked to the river and wrote to Ruth there. Clover and cattle and she-oaks and brown water . . . Dreadfully tired until sunset (good one). Bucked up and made rather a nice little rhyme . . .
Thursday *September 7*	Rode out with Eric and Mr Dewhurst, moved sheep from Racecourse to Emu. Hot thundery day, pinky iridescence in the clouds, blue haze and mirages everywhere (lagoons with trees). Afternoon: Rode with "Old Hoppy" (Jim Steves) to take bullocks out of Lloyds to Emu. Nice old man, gentle and shy . . . Looked at all the dams. Seven solid hours riding. Very sleepy and contented . . .
Saturday *September 9*	Mail brought lots of letters and books, and a request for permission to print "My Country" in an Anthology in England (addressed Miss Dorothea Mackellar, Poetess, Sydney, Australia)! . . .

KURRUMBEDE — MUSWELLBROOK

Friday *September 15*	Good journey but horrid, hot-wind day. No adventures. Made colour verses about Australia nearly all the time . . .

MUSWELLBROOK — SYDNEY

Saturday *September 16*	. . . Nice to be home. Wrote to Robin and copied out verses—most of which I'd carefully left at K'bede. Bed late. Drunk with sleep.
Sunday *September 17*	. . . Ruth came. We talked, it was a comfort—at least I don't know if she felt it so, the dear, but I did. And by and by I walked across the park with her when the sky was peacock blue and all the stars were out. She likes my new verses—I'm so glad . . .
Thursday *September 21*	I was going to dressmaker's and two garden parties and a Ball but Mother had an "inspiration". Bless her heart! It was that I should stay quite quiet and have Ruth to play with, which was done, and very nice it was . . .
Saturday *September 23*	. . . Dentist. Was a miserable coward. Nerves are petering out altogether . . . I got a letter from Robin. Felt restless. Sewed a little, typed a little, wrote a line

OPPOSITE: *The Station Boundary* A.H. Fulwood

or so, and R. came and we talked, and then the dear Milnes turned up, and of course we laughed ourselves helpless. R. stayed on and we had a short but sweet acting time down in my office . . .

Sunday
September 24

. . . To-day I went into my old room at Dunara. It felt strange, so big, and so *dead.*

Tuesday
September 26

. . . Dentist. Rested, read Wells' *Mr Polly.* Clever, amusing, vulgar and quite immoral, I suppose! He deserts his wife and commits arson and one doesn't mind a bit . . . Dr Thring won't be back till Friday—this waiting rather gets on one's nerves.

Wednesday
September 27

Went out motoring with Ruth, in the rain. Went to South Head and back along Bondi to Maroubra Bay and laughed and did ourselves good. Evening: Did skipping and tidied cupboards energetically . . . Translated some more of the 5th *Canto (Inferno).*

Friday
September 29

. . . The Child didn't come (thank Heavens!) I am to go to hospital on Sunday and Dr Thring will see me on Monday . . .

On October 1 Dorothea entered The Terraces, a private hospital established in 1903 by her father's friend Alexander MacCormick. She is never explicit about the nature of her operation. For some months before this date the diaries contain swastikas (her secret symbol for menstruation) in ever-increasing frequency. The operation was not a hysterectomy (she underwent this later in life), but, most probably, a procedure designed to arrest excessive menstrual bleeding.

LIVERPOOL ST. — THE TERRACES

Sunday
October 1

. . . Nervous feeling. Said goodbyes (servants rather tearful and everybody else in studiously high spirits) and arrived at my cheerful room with Mother and Dad. Poor dears—When they went away it was less strain. The nurses all seem very nice and pretty, and the view from the window is lovely. Only you can't see that from the bed. I went to bed after lunch and was gradually prepared. I don't feel well—but all that is going to end.

Chilly work, waiting to be called to the theatre—only I don't think I was *very* nervous.

Chloroform is choky stuff and the pain and sickness after are beastly. I didn't "come to" properly till about 12. Four hours—Agh—the rest isn't a nice dream. No sleep.

Same as yesterday—not that I am writing this on the day. No sleep and no relief except the morphia. Mother came and I couldn't speak.

Better. The family came, including Eric, and I tried to laugh, of course. Disastrous failure—shrieked and wept bitterly, which upset the poor dears. They couldn't stay long. People have been sending lovely flowers.

. . . Slightly less painful to laugh now, but it still hurts abominably. They took the stitches out, and that isn't pleasant, but it's far from being the torture I was told of . . . 12 and 14 stitches. Quite little cuts.

Robin came. I felt ill and tired, worse luck . . . Meg and other nice visitors, but I'm pretty weak and they do knock me out. People send masses of the loveliest flowers—roses and lilies-of-the-valley and stocks and peonies, sweet peas and carnations—especially red roses. I do love them. The room is literally *full* of flowers, on every available niche.

Can turn over now. Same old morning. Oh, I'm hatefully weak, but the afternoons are stronger and the time passes. Only they are going to stop me having so many visitors. Nurse Alison is beautiful and a dear. She sometimes comes in at night and talks to me. Norman Pilcher came today. Got through it all right—and I *had* promised—only it was rather a strain for both of us.

Getting on slowly. Jim came and Florence and others —Ruth (her **man* in attendance**) brought flowers, the dear—so did the others.

R. came before he went away to Melbourne. Horrid saying goodbye—which is absurd—I don't want to get over-tired and put things back. They say that does happen—sometimes.

man: Reginald "Rex" Sessions Barrett. The fact that Dorothea refers to Ruth's "man" in code suggests that this is a new, or clandestine, relationship.

Tuesday *October 17*	Went out on the veranda (in Nurse Edwards' arms) for an hour. Abominably tired all day. But the garden *was* beautiful to see! Red roses came for me.
Wednesday *October 18*	Of the day there is nothing memorable, but massage began in the evening—very gently—with Lyd and Nurse Alison, and I did laugh so! . . .
Thursday *October 19*	**R. came back straight from the train** . . .
Friday *October 20*	. . . A better day than yesterday—which was *vile.* Lots of visitors, including Peggy and N.P. I wish men didn't get upset when one is tired—and oh *dear* I *was* tired. More laughing massage . . .
Sunday *October 22*	. . . Mother, and Meg, and Ruth after lunch. Felt very cheerful. **I can't help being glad that R. loves my figure.** Not a bit tired . . .
Wednesday *October 25*	. . . Got up in the afternoon for a little while, and developed an appalling backache, which got worse and worse while various visitors were here. At last Ruth hustled me into bed with various nurses, and hot water bottles, and it eased off in time, but I couldn't read or think . . . Massage in the dark. Ugh — that pain!
Thursday *October 26*	Very limp. Refused to see N.P. and others in the afternoon, and was far too tired to get up, tho' the pain has not come back. R. came, was rather a dear, **but I *can't* stop him making love to me now—I don't wonder.** It must be hard for a man when a girl is so quiet and yet—just waking up, and I can't change myself in that way. Mother came, and Del. No one else but Dr Thring for a nice long yarn, interrupted by The Child. However was too tired for him and sent him away . . .
Saturday *October 28*	R. came. Was studiously distant and cheerful till the end when—**when I lay limp and scarcely realized how close things were.** Afternoon: Got up. Mother and Ruth could not come. I wrote to R. on the balcony . . . and wept bitterly as I have not done for three years. It did me good.

OPPOSITE: *Roses* Tom Roberts

THE TERRACES — LIVERPOOL ST.

Monday
October 30

Goodbyes and Dr Thring . . . Got up and packed. Oh the weary business! More goodbyes. I really was sorry to go and Mother came and I felt faint — Home, and thankfully undressed. Good to be with the family again.

Wednesday
November 1

. . . Drove a little, and N.P. came, and then I went to bed at 5.30 according to orders and was *not* tired. Glorious change! He's awfully kind, but oh — I *couldn't*.

Saturday
November 4

. . . Went for drive (waterlilies in the Park very lovely). Came back quite soon and went straight to bed. Lay in the dark till at last my headache was better. The dear Mother —like a dove at its best.

Sunday
November 12

. . . Wrote "Spring Song".

LIVERPOOL ST. — KURRAJONG HEIGHTS

Thursday
November 16

. . . Scorching day. Train (met Ruth and the dearest Dad came in the train too —) to Parramatta, where we met Mother and the car. Hot, *terribly* hot drive. Arrived at Kurrajong Heights. It is a dreadful hill (from the motorists' point of view) and the sulky was waiting to take me up because of the shaking . . .

Friday
November 17

. . . Lay in the garden (cool day), went for a small—such a small walk! Only down to the garden gate. They slung my hammock between a pine and a pittosporum on the slope overlooking the glorious orange orchard that climbs the hill, and a nice and too affectionate dog came and played with us . . . A very little acting.

Saturday November 18

. . . Nearly dressed before breakfast! Went out to hammock afterwards, carrying writing materials but not seriously intending to write. Laughed a great deal . . . Began a new play inside and continued it satisfactorily on the lawn.

Monday November 20

All the morning we played in the hammock and the play developed most amazin'! Afternoon: More play, and a little walk down the orchard by the Sarsaparilla vines and under the apple trees . . .

Hammock. Little pinky-yellow apricots. Scores of different kinds of singing birds. Seven nice letters. Acting.

It is too happy a time for me to write much.

. . . A walk in the wild wet woods. Brown fern and pinky red leaves and coppery-gold—and waratahs and many sorts of loveliness and great grey veils of blowing rain. And a splendid dark purple storm down in the plain. Acted.

Acted by the hammock and things went rapidly. Ate wild cherries—all the days are alike and each one different — I slept out in the hammock all night long, and it was wonderful, and the dawn was clear, red and honey colour and the mist a calm sea over the plain.

And the moon set late.

Pouring rain. Wrote a letter or two, made Carol die. Afternoon: Acted Puritan play, getting D'Ossory into a bad hole. Evening: Same. Went well.

. . . I shall hate going away tomorrow and Ruth is not coming down, which makes it worse. Evening: Sat on the grass in the moonlight and yarned — and felt sad. Slept out in the hammock.

KURRAJONG HEIGHTS — SYDNEY

Awfully hot day. Played under the pine trees with Ruth all the morning, and Mother came for me, and Janet Stephen arrived to bear Ruth company. Got lemons—enormous things as big as Mac's fist—and came down through the lovely country, which grew hotter mile by mile—and after Parramatta there were constant flocks of sheep, and we *were* so tired, so when we got home we undressed and then I wrote out plays.

Bed—*very* good.

Although Dorothea has made no earlier mention of a forthcoming trip to England, at the beginning of December she suddenly begins preparations to leave Sydney with her parents in the New Year. Her father would shortly be formally commissioned by Lord Chelmsford, the Governor of New South Wales, to "enquire into the treatment of delinquent and neglected children in Great Britain and the Continents of Europe and America, and to recommend for adoption whatever measures you may consider might with advantage be introduced into the State of New South Wales".

Saturday *December 2*	. . . Wrote many letters, including one informing H.H.C. of our departure . . .
Monday *December 4*	. . . All the silver was packed today . . .
Tuesday *December 5*	Photographer. Very hot day . . . Dentist and Doctor. By the way, he hurt quite a lot without reducing me to shivers. I *must* be better . . . Evening: Typed. Very tired. And Mother kept on washing palms, bless her, and the light flashed and flashed in my eyes.
Wednesday *December 6*	. . . Mr Nicholas came, and we had a good talk. I'm afraid it was mainly about my verse, which he doesn't want me to leave. He said A. G. Stephens* wrote nice things about it, but I haven't seen them. **He also told me things that make me think The Child is a liar**—but **then he's not normal.**
Saturday *December 9*	. . . Tidied up jewel-cabinet for packing. Ruth came. Acted a very little and talked a lot . . .
Monday *December 11*	Hottest day . . . (Wrote to my two R.'s.) Evening: Read, and on looking up a plagiarism in *Harpers'* ("Helen's Lips",* put bodily in the *Lone Hand*) found to my horror that **The Child had cribbed** two things in the same month—word for word. I don't know what I ought to do, and he did the same with a French play.
Tuesday *December 12*	Did not sleep very well—went out early shopping. Then Ruth came. I am growing to live for that, which is folly (but sweet) . . . Went to bed very early and slept so badly.

Stephens: Alfred G. Stephens, writer, critic and editor.
"Helen's Lips": a poem by Frederic Knowles.

OPPOSITE: *Girl in a Hammock* Jane Sutherland

Wednesday *December 13*	. . . Looked up that cribbed verse at the Public Library, unsuccessfully . . .
Friday *December 15*	Went to say goodbye to Lili (and she said I hear **you've broken poor Norman's heart**—oh dear, those McPhillamys!). Then with Ruth for a bathe at Bronte. It was lovely, especially at the end when we went in the surfy part . . .
Saturday *December 16*	R. rang up to say her Mother was worse, so she could not come. I was sorry. Horrid day—terrific hot wind with clouds of dust that hurt my eyes all day. Shopped most successfully and smashed Mother's letter opener by my own d. clumsiness as soon as ever I got home, and I know I shan't be able to get her another as nice, for I got the nicest in the shop! . . .
Monday *December 18*	Mrs Bedford had a good night, so they aren't quite so worried . . .

Wednesday   December 20

Glorious blue-gold day . . . Bathe at Rose Bay with R. They wouldn't let us in the Women's Bath, saying the men's was "continental and respectable, all right" . . .

Thursday   December 21

Cold too bad to go bathing. I felt so stupid and slack. Washed hair and sat in the sun. Tied up presents. Afternoon: Abigail Child came, looking well and awfully glad to see a friend . . . Poor dear. She's at Prince Alfred's now and likes it . . .

Friday   December 22

. . . Went bathing with Ruth to Bronte. As she said, it was the nicest bathe for water that we had ever had. High tide and miraculously clear waves . . .

Sat on the roof in the sun to get my cold better. Afternoon: Florence. When I left her we went to ask for Mrs Bedford. She had just died that minute— Mrs Brady told me that Dorothy Owen **had cut her own father** deliberately twice and threw a man over because he was poor, and it's horrid, and I had no defence except that she used not to be like that . . .

Packed books, wrote Christmas letters . . . Afterwards went to Ruth. She (and the others) very brave and self-possessed. White as ghosts. It *was* merciful, though—Came home late . . .

. . . Town. Did everything I wanted to . . . Home, and a nice talk with Dad **(about his knighthood, which will be announced in a few days)**. He hasn't told anybody else . . .

. . . Went to the Gardens to R. and saw a placard hanging on the railings in front of S. Mary's:

> *"You millionaires who tread on air*
> *Remember, Authors' poorly fare*
> *And if you question how and why*
> *You read this and you do not buy.*

The best verses written on the late Cardinal. They are disposed here because the author has no other way of bringing them to your notice."

Followed a lot of printed verse which I hadn't time to read . . . Evening: Just us. All very tired . . . No New Year resolutions.

The Grand Tour 1912-13

It was a grey hot day. We went to early church, Mother, Mac and I. Lilian came to lunch. There was a sense of goodbye over everything . . . and then I was called to the telephone about father's K.B. The *Herald* and *Telegraph* wanted photographs and interviews. I gave both, but Mother wasn't to know till morning. **She doesn't want it any more than I do, but he wants it for her, so we must be very glad.** I went to bed early, being tired out, and Mac rang up afterwards with the news, got from an evening paper.

Monday January 1 1912

Went and congratulated mother, who was rather—shocked. Dad came home, and piles of letters for him came by the first post. I joined R. in town and we motored out to Diamond Bay. It was a perfect blue and gold day, and we climbed right down to the sea and sat on the rocks with our feet dabbling in the adorable little rainbow-coloured pools, and talked, and tried to act, but all the play-people had not exactly died but gone far away. However, we did call some of them back. Sleepy and happy. It was a good day.

Tuesday January 2

Rather a scramble, and we went to see Aunt Effie, and then there were many visitors—all nice. In the evening I wrote twelve letters for Dad—he is getting hundreds. Such nice ones, saying splendid things—and they *all* sound sincere.
  But the going away is beginning to hang over us.

Wednesday January 3

. . . Dr Bennet and N.P. and shopping and letters, all in the morning and all rather a strain. More letters and *most* visitors in the afternoon. I did forty letters that day and nearly reached the end of my tether.

Thursday January 4

Slackened work except for odds and ends of packing and hair washing. Frightfully hot day. Worn out to the point of tears. Ruth came. I lay flat on the floor, and she sat there, and we talked of our meeting in England . . . nearly 9 years ago . . . She is a brave dear. And then we lunched on the *Orama* and a great storm came on, and I went back and rested till people came. Lots and lots of goodbyes.

Friday January 5

OPPOSITE: *Summer* Margaret Preston

R.M.S. ORAMA

Saturday January 6

Hurry and restlessness. The usual nightmare on the ship . . . People had sent heaps of glorious flowers. Alison Hanna a great mass of white water-lilies. Presently, while writing letters for Dad, I found I had forgotten a lot of cards, so sent a wireless for them—feeling rather dashing. Bishop Frodsham* of North Queensland at our table—or rather we at his. I rather like him. Two adorable nuns and the rest mostly scrubs, snobs and swabs, but one can't really sort them out, of course. They are nearly all from interstate. This is a magnificent ship, far the nicest I ever saw, and it is a beautiful day **and I miss the boys horribly.**

Sunday January 7

The day made up of writing letters, reading A. T. Strong's *Peradventure* and Ransom's *Storytelling* and making friends with the two nuns. One French and the other German . . . They are both sweet Ladies of Grace. The Bishop knew Oscar Wilde and Richard Le Gallienne, the latter was at school with him. "I kicked that boy," he said thoughtfully, "more than I've kicked anyone—mainly for hanging round girls' schools. I was a prefect at that time—He was extraordinarily good-looking—Wilde took a great fancy to him. But I was a young Philistine and W. depressed me. *That* was at Cambridge—" And so on. Then he took me up on the boat deck while he sent a Marconigram. It was rather thrilling, up there in the dark and wind, and there was *such* a 'normous dazzling blue spark. It's a very powerful whatsisname.

MELBOURNE

Monday January 8

Cold at first, and H.H.C. came down to the boat and there was the usual scurry about luggage. I didn't go off with him for fear of disappointing Nursie.* He is very much as I had pictured him, only less tall. We saw Nursie and then

---

Frodsham: George Horsfall Frodsham, Bishop of North Queensland 1901–13.
Nursie: Dorothea's childhood nurse.

I went to lunch with the Champions and Mr Strong, who was nice, and more nervous than even I. We talked hard. I was dreadfully tired and glad to get back to the Oriental Hotel a little before Lorna Smith came. It was very hot by then. Lorna looked strong and cool and brown. She had a delightful floppy hat of green straw and white plaited together. We could not talk very well, there was too much to say.

The knavish luggage man was seven hours late, which gave point to the jest about Porters in the pantomime that evening . . .

MELBOURNE — ORAMA

. . . Caught the train by the skin of my teeth to find Nursie . . . on board, and glorious flowers and letters yet more welcome — **poor old Nursie has been so unhappy**! That sort of arrangement never works. They are not kind to her. We were very sad about it all. The ship went out at 3 p.m. Letters and rest.

Wednesday January 10

Stayed in bed, so did M. Not ill but pessimistic. Read Plutarch. A sailor was smashed against a bulwark by a heavy sea—killed.

Sunday January 14

Reached Fremantle at 10. Suddenly it was fearfully hot and we needed all the punkahs. Did not go ashore, wrote many letters, and rested. In the evening I felt alive for the first time since leaving home. It was warm and **I wore Robin's red roses** and was gay . . .

Tuesday January 16

. . . After dinner listened to Bishop Frodsham and laughed helplessly. He tells yarns very well. (They were dancing on deck and the music drove my brain wild, but I don't like any of these more or less puffy youths well enough to stand and hope they'll ask me—it always *is* suggestive of a slave market— so I kept away altogether.) . . . He said the men of his diocese call him The Bloody Bishop when they feel fond of him and *that* bloody Bishop when they're annoyed . . . There's a horse racing in the North called His Lordship. Last year two wires were run together with this effect: "The Bishop of North Queensland is suffering from a severe attack of fever. His Lordship is scratched from all events." . . .

Wednesday January 17

Also: an advertisement in a Townsville paper the other day (sent to *Punch*):

after an account of the rescue of a horse from a flooded creek, they said the owner's name is not known, but he has three white fetlocks and is branded XY4 on the near shoulder.

He should be easy to recognise.

And: Townsville Essays on what Boys and Girls can do for Australia. There was a long account of boys' activities and then: "A girl cannot do much for Australia but she can do her best."

"My favourite book is Little Nell of London. Little Nell was a gurl but what she said, she done it."

In answer to his Natural History question, by the son of the local shoemaker who was, of course, a Radical: "The male Ant is a Useless creature and may be likened to the Nobility and Clergy." . . .

Friday *January 19*	Wrote a few letters and a few rhymes, read *The Trobador Poets*—charming book. **Robin sent it to me** and I only got it yesterday . . . and met a nice red-haired girl artist called Edith Anderson. The Bishop introduced us because she is in the 2nd class. We had a tremendous talk about creative work in Australia . . . In the evening we had a happy giggling circle . . . but I had a horrid headache, and I wasn't in tune with all those nice people.
Saturday *January 20*	It passed so quickly! I got up late, after a watermelon breakfast in bed, and everybody seemed charming, and also, in the afternoon, the Chief Engineer took me all over the engine . . . He explained everything most patiently, and the turbine gauge fascinated me most—and he took me all over the stoke holes, too. The stokers stared as if I was a ghost. Likewise I saw the electric steering gear—this is the first ship to have it.
Sunday *January 21*	Got up for 7 o'clock communion and was thoroughly tired. Rested and enjoyed the rest of the day . . . Resisted the blandishhments of Burke* and others who wanted me to be a page at their bridal party on the night of the Fancy Dress Ball. It was quite hard to do, though of course the thing was out of all question. Irish people are so persuasive . . .

Burke: Edmund Burke, Canadian bass, one of Nellie Melba's favourite singers and returning to London after singing with Melba during her 1911 Melbourne season.

Heard that the *Carmen* opera costumes were to be brought up from the hold, so gave up my idea of going as a Spaniard. Collected cigar bands and brown paper and with Mary's eager help made up a tobacco dress, fan, and jewellery pasted on to my neck and arms, and effective crown of red-gold and tobacco leaves. The bridal party was the choice of the evening, but I *was* glad I didn't join! Mrs Burke was splendid as the bride, Mrs Hawkins lovely as a sailor-flapper, and Nina Mylne and Mrs Cheeke looked very well. **She tells me the Nokes** were **low and broad**, like the table decorations. Mrs Hawkins took the breath away, and Mr Forsayth, the King of the Cannibal Islands as a small boy! . . . It was awfully hot but great fun. I didn't mean to dance, but succumbed. Miss Garrard was a charming little Apache girl, by the way, and *all* the costumes reached a very high level. The nicest part of the evening was a long smoking-talk with Sir Stanley Bois in the comp-aratively cool dark . . .

Tuesday   January 23

. . . I won the sweep—first prize 3 guineas! It staggered me, somehow. I am generally so unlucky. Before I forget, here is the Townsville boy's essay on Melba. He is the son of the local hotel keeper, and Melba had not behaved prettily there. "Madame Melba is the most wonderful singer in the world. But she is not beautiful; she has not a good figure, and she is not at all a lady."

. . . The sea is a marvellous lapis lazuli blue . . . There are great beams of pale blue light, rayed like the wriggles in watered silk, going deep down below the surface, and the surface itself is fretted with the delicatest cross-cut ripples, all sorts of marvellous patterns you can scarcely distinguish—how exquisitely soft the breeze must be! The sunsets are wonderful now, thin sharp greens and oranges with a very brilliant little silver boat of a moon sailing through it all.

I love bathing in the phosphorus at night—in the dark—blazing stars and trickles of flame over my body.

Wrote long letters to Ruth and others . . . At night, after nearly everybody had gone to bed, Burke and Ciccolini* sang for us. It was *heavenly*. They sang a lot, ballads and things out of *Tosca* and *Bohème* and *Hérodiade*. Sir Stanley

Ciccolini: Guido Ciccolini, a tenor who had sung with Melba during her 1911 Melbourne season.

accompanied them, which was rather wonderful of him. They got awfully worked up. Cicc. acted like mad, and was chuckling the next moment. Burke made a superhuman effort to keep still and gripped the piano. They went so fast too. Sir S. said it was the hardest day's work he'd ever done and with all that voice in his ear he couldn't think!

COLOMBO

Thursday January 25

. . . Nice brown babies! Nice white little humped hillocks, and yellow stucco walls, and red roads, and lolling palms and burning blue sky! Dinner at the Galle Face Hotel in the cool, with the sound of the sea all round us. Bought star sapphire, and all went home dead tired. **It was not a happy day at all. Three had bad headaches, Dad was uneasy. He's the worst traveller I know and I haven't** proper hold of the reins yet. There were hitches—I'll do better by and by.

Friday January 26

. . . We have a new table companion. Red hair that used not to be so, and an immense anxiety to show that she has travelled. She tells one three times in each course that she always went by P & O before . . .

Sunday January 28

The Bishop preached a good sermon on Realities. Also he stumbled into the wrong sea service and read part of the thanksgiving after a Naval Battle . . .

Monday January 29

. . . Stewards' concert at night. "Our motto is Comicality without Vulgarity." Help! They didn't leave much to the imagination . . . The Bishop got Nina, Edith Anderson and me to the front row, where I sat with my legs coiled up, and my head in Nina's lap at the startling bits. At the end it came on to rain—soaking, pouring rain . . .

The Rajah follows me round with his soft, black eyes and his soft oily voice—but no doubt he is very nice.

Tuesday January 30

. . . We passed Guardafui in the afternoon—such a great jagged cape . . . Long conversation with the Mr Rome, who only barked before. All about Egypt *and* marriage, if you please! . . . Jumble games in the evening. Not bad fun, but the moon on the upper deck was better. Limericks, hat pin and peas, grab, passengers' names, etc. All this time I have been growing into friends with Nina.

Read Conrad's *Under Western Eyes*. . . Mr Rome played a very fine game of deck-quoits. **It is absurd—he's making a dead set at me.** He danced eagerly and talked for hours in the moonlight on the upper deck—with and without Nina, and he talks down to me, nice old thing, and **he said I had an innocent face**! Never have I been treated as such an ingénue before.

RED SEA

. . . Joined in a skipping contest (endurance) and came second. 143. Hard work, for the ship was rolling very violently. The slim Todman flapper did 197! . . .

Sports and cricket matches and avoidance of **Mr Rome**, until evening when that was not possible any more. Fancy Dress Dinner Dance and Gymkhana. People usually wore operatic costumes, and looked extremely well. Nina wore a white wig and black hat, patches and rouge, and looked simply ripping. Mr Garrard very attractive as Trilby. I wore a semi-oriental gipsy dress (from Traviata with additions of my own) and it looked well, so about forty of the passengers told me. I'm thinking they mostly were of the opinion of the Cannibal Island man, who said, "You look quite different to-night, absolutely charming. I didn't know you!" Mary lent me a crimson silk tie with which to bind my head. The dress was a tunic of gauzy greenery-yallowy stuff with tiny Magyar sleeves embroidered in red sequins like the stiff dark-blue broidered band across the breast: there was a quaint short red-sequinned zouave jacket, and a stiff skirt of any mixed rainbow of colours, tied round the hips with a fringed scarf of dull cream that had crimson roses on it. As I wore the golden Spanish shawl, crimson roses, green macaws and all, between the dances . . . I was rather like a macaw myself. I wore no stays, but just now my waist is springy and muscular, so it didn't matter. **Mr Rome** was rather trying, though he *is* a good sort . . . **he kept on suggesting marriage more or less scotchly**—Oh dear! . . .

SUEZ

A perfect day, very cold and bright. The doctor came on board, and swarms of hawkers. I just *had* to buy one lovely ostrich feather. Talked to Edith and wrote to Ruth—for we got many letters from England, among them one from Charlie Bean saying that Alston Rivers [Dorothea's English publisher] had accepted *The Little Blue Devil*, on good terms. I *was* surprised, and full of suppressed excitement. It's awfully good of Charlie, he is taking a lot of bother about it.

The sunset was most exquisite, lovely shades of lilac, primrose and orange, crimson lake and dull blue, and seagulls lay on the lakes like water lilies. I wanted four eyes. The searchlight at night was beautiful too, but *oh* the cold! Nina and I had to walk hard, and finally we took refuge in the warm recess of the smoking room and smoked cigarettes . . .We were joined by the Bishop and Burke, both highly amused and amusing on the young men and maidens of the top deck, huddled under rugs and alert for chaperons. *I* think it was much tamer than in my young days, and N. and I went up on purpose to look! Early bed—but couldn't sleep, for we reached Port Said at 1 a.m. and a most infra dig row began.

The following morning Dorothea and her parents left the Orama. *Their plan was to explore, by means of a well-organised tour, some of the antiquities of Egypt.*

PORT SAID — CAIRO

Early rising and delay over luggage. Goodbyes—I really am sorry to leave this nice pleasant ship—and on shore to a hotel where we drowsed through a morning. **I wasn't well and the hurrying hurt me.** Train, first through desert—white sand and stuff like saltbush—and then leagues of fertile Sudd. Canals (eau-de-nil—lovely soft colour) with friezes of graceful figures all along them—slim blue-gowned men and black-gowned women, and supercilious camels loaded with incense, and resigned donkeys loaded with half the world, and children just like all other children. And creamy flat-roofed towns with swirling writing stuccoed on the walls. Then Cairo and the Savoy, which is gorgeous

OPPOSITE: Sir Charles and Dorothea in Moorish costume

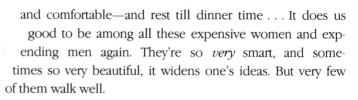

and comfortable—and rest till dinner time . . . It does us good to be among all these expensive women and expending men again. They're so *very* smart, and sometimes so very beautiful, it widens one's ideas. But very few of them walk well.

Wednesday February 7

Pyramids and Sphinx—with a deep, burning blue sky behind them. Dromedaries are rather nice to ride, much more cushiony than they look. But they make the most hideous noise—far worse than anyone told me!—bubbling and creaking and snarling and hissing. Yesterday in the bazaars we saw some beautiful Egyptian ladies, with white-rose skins and chestnut hair under their white veils, buying things and giggling even more than other girls. I got red slippers there and was drunk with the colour and the bustle and the scent—yes and the smell. Carpets and brasses, and sweetmeat sellers and jewel-merchants, and slipper sellers and beggars, *hajjis* [pilgrims] and *Bedawi* [Bedouins]—ooh! Mother and I prowled about looking for hats, without much success—heaps of oppressively smart and no doubt staggeringly expensive French shops, with yard-long plumed erections in their windows, but no travelling hats.

As for the Sphinx, I *can't* write of it, it's too wonderful.

Thursday February 8

Lazy writing morning, walked about and admired the beautiful private houses—palaces. Went to the Museum and saw all the jewellery and the tomb-furniture . . . The mummies were rather ghastly—one priest is writhed as if in awful agony, her head turned on her shoulder and her little feet drawn up—I wonder whether she is the one that is said to haunt the Museum? The mummied gazelle is rather pathetic—and the wee plump child still bound in the funeral clothes — I rather hated the sacred rams, all covered with gold leaf. Their foolish faces looked full of the *awfulness* of stupidity, the stupidity that murders, and I thought how they lived in luxury that they didn't appreciate while the fellahini [peasants] sweated and bled and starved and died in their millions—and I think that we're still rather like that! The fine bulldog that lives here in the Savoy and goes out for an airing in his car is a better animal than a sacred ram, but after all it's rather sickening that his daily expenses would support a family for a week—putting it moderately.

Afterwards Mother and I went for a drive alone, through a misty amber sunset, to Old Cairo, and a man took us down through a huge old gate into a vile passage to see the Church of Abu Sargah. But ophthalmic and villainous-looking persons pressed round, and it was getting dark and the way grew longer and longer. So we turned back, in spite of his excited lowerings of the charge. He began to swing-to the great door—8 inches thick and covered with embossed copper—and for one second M. and I both thought we were going to be locked in, and I think our hearts gave the same sickening leap. But I put my foot in the door very quickly, saying "Yes? An old door?" and he replied sulkily that it *was antika*—and a beggar at the gate laughed loudly and pointed at him. I have never heard a more expressive and annoying laugh. It said, "Yah! You thought you had a gold mine, and it is trickling through your fingers!" So we piastre'd him somewhere within a shilling and went home.

CAIRO — ASYUT

Dressed, packed and had breakfast in 20 minutes. Rather a scramble to the train, but the most interesting train journey I have ever had . . . There was always something fresh to see, and most of all I loved the mud towns with their date palms—lumpy and bumpy and feathery, all sprouted out of the ground like mushrooms. And I was haunted by the concluding line of a verse that I can't trace—"My shady city of palm-trees"—and it annoyed me because it makes "palm-trees" a spondee, which it isn't.

Saturday February 10

Lots of shawl sellers at Asyut. I got Mother a beauty for a birthday present, but of course, it's fearfully heavy. I rather loved a green and silver one, but — . . .

Early next morning they boarded the paddle-steamer Ramses which was to take them up the Nile as far as Aswan, 550 kilometres from Asyut.

Sunday February 11

Perfect day—opal sunrise and clear, cool air. The banks

are continually changing. Little boys and girls running along strip off their one garment and shout out that they are the Adams and Eves in the Paradises, but the *Ramses*, obedient to the Regulations, throws no *bakshish*. We passed Abydos and, yesterday, Roda, where Antinous was drowned.

Great limestone cliffs, dazzling white with tombs of wolves and crocodiles cut in them. Hawk's tail, crescent-shaped. Bare mountains, fawn-coloured, with lilac shadows — . . .

DENDERAH

*Monday
February 12*

The morning slid away like nothing, with *dahabeeyahs* [large sailing boats] and wonderful changing scenery, and at lunchtime we reached Denderah and rode to the temple there . . . There are several cartouches of Nero, as well as the great bas-relief of Cleopatra and Cesarion on the outer wall—but it is very magnificent, and the work is most delicate, especially the carving and colouring in the crypt. There is a splendid view from the roof (a few years ago there was a whole village of mud huts on it), and they are still excavating at the sides, bits of temples, great solid hewn stone, showing out of the fine brown earth. The workmen go to and fro at a jogtrot, chanting. Hundreds of little birds are nesting in every crevice of the huge walls.

The Copts—the very early Copts—used part of Denderah as a church, and they painstakingly defaced every bit of carving that they could reach or had time for. It must have taken years. So all the lower figures are chiselled away, only the delicate detail of the thrones and head dresses remain. The crypt is untouched, and some of the figures of Hathor . . . Moon-Goddess, Lady-of-Love . . . are whole except where they have hacked her beautiful breasts. I know the destroyers were Christians by that sign. A Mahommedan would have attacked impartially. Some of the Divine Blue, her colour, is stretched over the ceiling with the gold stars shining out of her garment.

The little birds are nesting, and they sing so busily in Hathor's House.

Luxor at night. A row of roofs and a cluster of tall columns against the sky.

*Tuesday
February 13*

We left early in the morning and were ferried across the river of Thebes. It was quite a long ride to the Tombs of the Kings, but the day was perfect,

with an absolutely cloudless blue sky. It was hot, very hot, and I loved it. My donkey was a beauty. Her name was Minniehaha (I think because the donkey boy believed me to be American) and she passed everything on the road, in spite of my efforts, as soon as ever we began any conversation . . . The Tombs are very fine, and so is Hatasa's temple. She built with an eye for a fine site, that queen . . . Coming home we passed the Colossi of Memnon. They are the only things not as I imagined them. I thought they were out in a lovely yellow desert by themselves, whereas they are quite close to the city, and not specially huge.

I would love to have been alone at the Tombs of the Kings, with the hawks and the Sun and the rocks and the delphinium blue sky. But **there was a little passenger and he immediately began to be slimy**—however, it didn't matter, really. We saw the mummies lying down there among their dream-pictures, and it seemed even crueller than when they were in a museum.

. . . That night, having a bad cold and being quite tired out, I dressed in dim green and silver and went to a dance at the Winter Palace Hotel with the doctor, whose name is Rossiter. It was great fun, though trying in a way, as one had to dance before a huge audience! The floor was good and the music fair. I danced with a clever London doctor-man called Hamil—an enormous person—6 foot 3, and quite six feet broad . . .

The dance *did* do my cold good.

The Doctor says that when they take these boats after their five months' rest, they find all sorts of gruesome things in the paddles—men's bodies no less—because people are always being pitched into the Nile, and nothing more is heard of them—and they drift down and are caught.

TEMPLE OF KARNAK

Wednesday February 14

It covers a thousand acres and you can't possibly take it in in one visit, but it is magnificent . . . The Hall of Columns is splendid. So is the view from the roof. You see all over the Nile and the desert, and the White Nile (which Mrs Ernest Cudmore spoonered into the Light Wine) of the road to the Tombs of the Kings . . .

In the late afternoon Mother and Dad and I went over to the Temple of Luxor . . . We saw where the Copts had plastered and painted the lovely walls (same as at Karnak) and we saw the Roman altar and Alexander's shrine and the statues of Ramses. I sat on his knee—a big slice of it that had fallen down—while we listened to the *muezzin* calling from the mosque nearby . . . The sky between the lotus columns was lilac and pansy purple and rose-pink, the columns almost black against it.

At Karnak there were scores of quite tiny boys, carrying baskets of earth from the excavations and singing a deafening chant, which grew louder as they met us.

Another very early start. I don't know which part of the day is loveliest. We went to the Rameseum and saw Ramses' Colossal statue—"My name is Ozymandias, King of Kings"—and his Pavilion, and the Temple of Der al Madinat, with the very beautiful Judgment Hall of Osiris. Ramses in battle . . . flinging his foes into the Orontes . . . returning in triumph, and waited on by naked ladies who fan him, and dance before him, and play draughts with him—all very jolly . . .

We left Luxor at noon and sailed on through perfect weather. It was most exciting going through the bridge at Esneh. We had only 10 inches to spare, and the men used themselves as fenders, in wild enthusiasm. When we got one paddle clear, a song of triumph began, which ceased abruptly as the other fouled. It ground and splintered, but no serious damage was done. It was horribly dangerous—for the men I mean. One of them was calmly walking along the face of the wall like a fly, with his back to the rail, and another continually dragged his legs out of the way only just in time, and if they had not swerved they would have been crushied [*sic*] like flies indeed. Or if they had dropped—the current was deadly swift and strong, and no power on earth could have saved them from being caught in the paddle. They love the excitement, and boast about it afterwards!

There was the most exquisite after-glow I have ever seen. I tried to write about it—like a fool. Silver and rose and nacre.

Saturday February 17

Another early start. A funny little white-painted train to Shellal, and then lovely *dahabeeyahs* sailing all in among the columns of Philae. Such beautiful columns, lotus and papyrus and palm. Then we rowed to the Dam, our boys singing all the time. One of them spent the waiting time playing a queer sort of tom-tom—half earthenware. Lunch and then . . . I watched them open the sluices—ooh! and then we went down to an accompaniment of naked bronzes diving and grinning for *bakshish*. By the way, the word for "greedy" is *Shakhat*. *Quys* = nice, *Quys ratia* = very nice, *Harrak Saida* = good morning, *Liltek Saida* = good evening, *Faloos* = money—and the rest I forget. Spelling phonetic—*mafish*—*malaish*, etc . . .

I forgot to say that that day at Thebes we saw the funeral of a woman, Coptic, I think, the body carried high on a bier, followed by a long crowd of black-robed mourners, wailing and beating their breasts, with tears streaming down their faces. The body was wrapped in a red shroud. Some brutes got down and took a photograph of the procession as it wound down from the hill.

ASWAN — KOM OMBOS

Monday February 19

Cruel, cold wind. Got up and saw the Crocodile God's temple before breakfast. Piles of mummied crocodiles there too . . . The Khamsin blew all day. If Father and I hadn't been feeling better we should have shrunk up altogether . . . There was less excitement getting through the lock this time—a very good passage, only we stuck on the worst sandbank in the river immediately afterwards. A rather interesting kind of man, whose name, it appears, is Mason, made friends with me over a piece of sugar-cane, and that evening tried to talk, but I was talking to Mrs Rawson instead. We changed cabins that night—Mother and I, I mean—and now we have singles, it's so nice.

Reached Karnak that night and saw a Coptic girl making Asyut shawls, twisting the silver wire with her bare fingers—poor little sleepy mite. Camels walking along the river bank like peacocks—trailing huge feathery bundles of sugar-cane.

LUXOR

I was going back to Karnak but felt ill again, too weak to do anything but visit the Luxor temple and stray about among the faded paintings in the East end of it. It's a most fascinating place. **Mr Mason took possession of me and immediately began to talk** confidentially. He said **I was unhappy**, and he meant it so kindly that I couldn't squash him. Besides he's jolly hard to squash. It really was one of the queerest conversations I have ever had . . . He said he could read me like a book! and so on, and so on . . . I can size him up so far, but I don't know quite how much is humbug yet. It appears he has been on board all the time, but I never saw him before yesterday. I rather think that he is ill. It amuses me to be treated in such a fatherly way—only a kid—and all that sort of thing—he's about 37 or 38 I suppose. The funny thing is that he sometimes says R.'s things, word for word, like a phonograph. Warnings about knocking myself about, spending strength and so on.

Tuesday
February 20

ABYDOS

. . . The temple there is the most beautifully decorated we have ever seen. *Beautifully* delicate work, with the colours as fresh and pure as if they were laid on today—but not as crude . . . We lunched in the forecourt of the Temple— which I didn't like . . . The blue-eyed man of understanding was *empressé*, not to say affectionate. He meant no harm, but I explained that one of the privileges of age (such as mine) was to accept endearments only when inclined for them. I think we understand each other on that point.

Wednesday
February 21

We rode to the 2nd temple that Ramses built . . . and then to a Coptic monastery—a venerable and dirty place, where a very beautiful priest read from their Bible in a melodious singsong, and they sold us leaves torn from a disused book . . .

Another talk with Mr Mason . . . I *think* he's entering on a rather violent flirtation with the laudable intention of distracting me from some imagined sorrow. I tell him I'm absolutely happy but he doesn't believe me.

Q. Do you know you are a beautiful woman?

A. No-o.

Q. Is that a new idea to you?

A. No, but I have always regarded it as a sign of defective judgment.

ASYUT

Reached Asyut early, as the ship hurried herself. Most of the passengers got off . . . Wrote some letters and said some goodbyes—and rode through the bazaars in the afternoon.

The moon is just beginning. She dances about in the smooth ripple like a curly silver fish.

A touching letter from Mr M. No, I'm a pig, it really was rather a nice one . . .

ASYUT — CAIRO

. . . Asyut is a pretty place, with lovely gardens and fine white houses and avenues of acacias. The poinsettias give it a homelike touch . . . Dusty, tiring journey, and then the Savoy and a letter from Ruth and clean, clean things and a heavenly sleep.

Washed my hair, it must be getting much thicker again, or it *couldn't* tangle so! Wrote to the boys and to Ruth, and in the afternoon went to the Agricultural Show with Dad. But to our sorrow we came just too late for the horses and cattle — "All go home—but you come here, perhaps you see two—or one." Those were gigantic black buffaloes who loved having their giant heads scratched with anything from the tip of a gloved finger to the ferrule of a parasol. We saw lots of lovely delicate-coloured silk being worn and heard a ripping Soudanese band with bagpipes and a hieratically proud drummer, and fell in love with a most exquisite brocade of gold and silver. Then home to Mother, and successful shopping afterwards. Silk stockings and an impertinent little French hat. Mother got one as well—light as feathers they are. And we looked at pretty shops and came home all three tired but happy, for Dad had acquired some very superior undergarments.

In the evening there was a dance here, all red coats and paint and feathers and glitter . . .

Sunday February 25 Went in to hug Mother for her birthday. Church. Sermon by the Bishop of London. He said one thing I thought good—that it is "not our attainments but our aims that settle our characters". Attainments are often accidental, but aims always leave a mark whether they materialise or not. Went to the Zoological Gardens in a happy hour. There were so many bird-and-beast babies there, including an elephant and a child hippopotamus who caught small potatoes and chewed them against (apparently) only two teeth . . .

Monday February 26 . . . They're selling branches of apricot blossom through all the streets . . . Missed Mr Mason when he called. I'd just gone to rest. **Do him good!**

Tuesday February 27 . . . Lazed, getting over my tiredness, and wrote to Ruth, **whose affairs are settled, thank God** . . . Motored out to Mena House to dine. It was a most beautiful night, and there was a moon. There was also **Mr Mason, who did his level best to get some conversation** and only succeeded in getting about 1 minute. But he made the most of his time, observing rapidly that **he loved me to distraction and I scared every man away**, and he'd cancel his passage if we were going to stay on there. He did his best to persuade Father, but of course, it wouldn't be convenient. He is *quite* mad, but kind . . .

Wednesday February 28 . . . Mother and I went to the Mosque of Amur with a casual and remarkably good-looking guide picked up on the way. Husein Ali. He showed us the pillars that no bad person can get through, and *I* got through with ease. They are polished smoother than any glass by the efforts of the faithful all these hundreds of years. Also the pillar that Mohammed commanded to go to Cairo from Mekka. At first it was disobedient and he had to hit it (mark of whip-lash etc.). The dear Mummy assured me afterwards, half-seriously, that she had not believed that . . .

After tea went calling with Mother. Such a glorious afterglow along the river— dusky scarlet.

And—little hollow tarts with strawberries set along in them in their juice— Créole—and peaches, each half set on a very spongy sponge cake, drenched in syrup, and other peaches served with chocolate sauce and vanilla ice (Russe).

And potatoes, creamy mash with grated cheese on their tops.

Fresh strawberries dipped in fondant.

Thursday February 29

. . . Wrote a rhyme about the bazaar and went to a sugar refinery at Hawamdieh with Dad. It's a French place, and they were making the loveliest sugar candy, as beautiful as diamonds—huge diamonds strung across bright copper bowls. Also sugar cones, millions of them being unshelled like white magic and a lovely chopping machine with a gentle voice that makes our white coffee dominos. Never have I gone through a refinery at such a pace . . . Went for a walk with Mother in the dusk to the gardens of the Place de l'Opéra. There was a Thé dansante in the Savoy, and there was gaiety everywhere—streams of motors and ostrich feathers and music and shining shops . . .

CAIRO — PORT SAID

Sunday   March 3

A sunny gay day, and we hated leaving. The manager pressed very nice chocolates on to us as we went off, and we ate them in the train instead of the rather horrid dinner. In Cairo everything was astir with the performance of *Aida* that was to take place at the Pyramids by moonlight. I did wish we could have stayed for it. The moon was simply glorious—a huge thing coloured like red corn—and afterwards she turned gay and mocking—

Scuttle for rooms at Port Said as the *Omrah* was late. Very bad accommodation, and dirty, but—but I rather liked sleeping in Port Said. It reminded me of early plays!

PORT SAID — OMRAH

Monday   March 4

She's a piggy little boat. Some of the passengers look nice, but it's such a short voyage, one has hardly energy to know them . . .

Tuesday *March 5*	Bitterly cold. Spent half the day in bed and the other half crouched in the scanty sunshine on the upper deck.
Thursday *March 7*	Naples at noon. It was bitterly cold and rather rainy, but Greek gods (young ones) were diving for pennies and rapscallions thrust up excessively long bamboos with bunches of violets and freesias on the ends . . . We went to the Museo and dazed ourselves with bronze and marble—a little bronze Victory from Herculaneum I loved. I'll get a copy of it some day, and the few Titians were beautiful, especially the Pope and his nephews, and also I loved *Hermes in Repose*, and a lovely head of a hooded Vestal Virgin . . . It's good to be speaking Italian again, and I haven't forgotten so very much.

Fifteen letters waiting, including a really nice note from H. G. Wells. How amused Ruth will be!

OMRAH — *ALGECIRAS*

Monday *March 11*	The first part of the day was long with delays and goodbyes. Delays because, owing to the coal strike, we simply *crawled.* Then we reached the dear Lion Couchant, and it was beautiful beyond words as we steamed across the bay in a clear green twilight that changed to blue. The broad band of lights round the base of Gibraltar were pinker and twinkled more than any I have ever seen, and the great harbour lights at the water's edge were yellow-white, like tropical stars . . . The Reina Cristina is a very beautiful hotel with a fountain in the patio of chequered marble, and a garden that I am longing to explore. There are orange trees. I can smell the blossom.

Letter from Mr Bean enclosing Alston Rivers' preliminary puff of Tony [*The Little Blue Devil*]. I *was* excited, for I never really thought he could get as far as print! The proofs are all done—that man is an angel (but I'd love to have had the joy of them myself, all the same). I wonder what sort of chapter headings he has given?

Tuesday *March 12*	A perfect day and a wonderful garden, full of great hedges of rose and lavender and rosemary and thyme, and nice high-curbed walls, and sunshine and oranges. I wandered about all alone and purring for pure joy, till the Parents came

down and we went for a walk over the old bridge and right out to the aquaduct. It was all pinks and greys and spring-greens. The women were washing clothes in the Guadiana down below, and the peach trees were coming into bloom and the plum trees into leaf. Various small boys on the aquaduct began to pester for pennies to buy oranges and Malaga sugar-cane, but gave it up as a bad job when I showed them my empty purse.

Algeciras is a climbing, twisting little cobbled town (that's all), but its ribbed tiles are a joy. I had forgotten how lovely their colours could be. Yellows and browns and pinks and greys, all exquisitely toned by the weather. I walked to the seashore and looked at Gib. There's a nice salty smell, and the wind is rising ominously.

Rode on donkeys to the Shrine of Our Lady of Lourdes, a long way round, and a short steep mule-track home. Heaps of wild lavender and amaryllis and broom. No trees but evergreen oaks (*encinas*) until we came to the river. It's a fascinating grotto and the miraculous water is delicious to taste.

In the afternoon Mother and I walked to the Moorish and Roman bridges and down into the Moorish quarter . . . After tea I freshened up so much that I went for a walk alone, down the goat-track at the side of the cliff, where earlier in the day, by the by, we had watched a magnificent golden eagle. He circled directly below us, gradually rising higher with his splendid wings quite motionless. You could count every feather in the tips, and he *did* look like the apotheosis of a monoplane. He rose till he was a black speck against the sun, far over our heads . . .

Well, I trod that goat-track to the Aso de la Caldera, and then it came on to rain. Oh the view was splendid! And the eagle flew to his nest just above me. But I climbed on the Aso and gathered amaryllis and had such a scramble down the south side. The rain was pouring by then. I took refuge in a wee cave, breathless—partly with excitement, and wet and chuckling. I felt rather like a fly on a wall. By and by the rain seemed to slacken, and I didn't want to be stuck in that lone eyrie while it grew dark, so I went on. It was such a long way back. I had to go down the Aso, there was no other way, and it was like a very tight chimney, and the rain rained, and I hung on with both hands and purred with excitement. At worst I knew I could climb back, but

I didn't want to. The rocks were wet and cold and very slippery, and the wind roared through that needle's eye, and the rain was dense and heavy all over the Vega. It looked as if it meant to go on till the end of the world. When I got to the cactus and pear trees it was wetter still, and all the lily stems were covered with active white snails. I broke through down to the river level and took refuge with a charming couple in a cottage. We made polite conversation for ages, and I believe they sent for an umbrella, but what with their patois and my broken Spanish, communication (communion?) was imperfect. They wanted to take me home, but they were just going to have dinner and I couldn't bother them. The man led me to the stepping stones, and they were rather alarming with the freshet that dashed between them. I felt like the heroine of a ballad crossing the wan water "where a man calls it Clyde".

> *"The neistan step that Elen took,*
> *The water reached her knee —"**

I hurried up past the mills, but some girls insisted I should come in and see the great stones turning in the sweet floury air. Brown flour. Then the rain began again, and I began to feel tired. Climbing by the Puerte de Cristo, a muleteer helped me, and then I had an interview with a dear old lady who had an umbrella—and some more conversations, but no more adventures till I got home, wet through, but *not* having spoilt my clothes, and with some magnificent memories of Ronda in the sun and the rain, as well as a bunch of Las Lagrimas de la Virgin.

Talked to the nice man with the white hair—we also watched the eagle together. Talked of suffragettes and cultivating the soil, and above all, London. He made me hungrier than ever for it.

On March 29, after visits to Granada and Málaga, Dorothea and her parents arrived in Seville.

Stayed in bed till lunchtime so as to feel well enough for the bullfight. [On

Sunday April 7

knee: From "Childe Waters", an old Scottish ballad.

OPPOSITE: *The Quay at Dinard* Ethel Carrick Fox

April 2 she had written: I was very ill. **Diarrhea, or dysentery.** Awful night.]
We went early and saw the great place (14,000 spectators) filling up. The
mantilla'd ladies made the boxes look very nice, especially when they spread
their *mantones* [shawls] over the front. The show opened with an amazing
punctuality, and the first great black bull came out at a swift run and immediately
killed a horse —What's the good of describing it? It has been done so many
times, and so well, and *I* can never forget. The only thing the descriptions
hadn't made me realize was the horrible passivity of the horses. One of the
picadores [horsemen] was injured, and I lost count of the murdered horses.
. . . Once the horses were out of the ring, I didn't mind watching at all.
Brutal, of course, but the bull was too angry to care. And what a critical
audience! They pardon no slip, and only applaud the best work.

Six bulls. Well, I never thought that I should be able to sit
it out, but as it was, and tired though I was, the afternoon did
not seem long.

But never another for either of us, as long as we live!

*The tour of Spain continued until at least April 17. The
journal for the period April 18 to June 19 is missing. A
verse book begun on September 11 1911 ended in Madrid
on April 13. The next, dated May 1, indicates that she had
arrived in London and was staying at 85 Jermyn Street. By this
time Ruth was also in London. Two months earlier Ruth had agreed
to marry Rex Barrett—apparently to everyone's surprise. In a letter dated March
4, Ruth wrote to Rex describing her family's disbelief at the news. The romance
seems to have foundered during the missing period of the journal. Perhaps
Ruth was sent to London to "get over it".*

LONDON — CAMBRIDGE

*Thursday
June 20*

In the morning I went to Alston Rivers as requested, and was interviewed—
an amusing business. If Mr Ellis' aim is to preserve the illusion of his being
an amateur, he succeeds in it to perfection . . . Caught the train with no time

to spare and had a nice journey down with R. The Bull Inn at Cambridge is a nice old Georgian place . . .

*Friday
June 21*

Wandered about and sat in gardens and went into ever so many churches. I counted 17 and there are lots more. In the afternoon we got a boat and rowed down the toy river, and rested under willow trees in the approved mode. It was lovely sliding under the bridges with a hush. Afterwards we went off into a sheltered path and acted Tony and Ann. It went well and in the evening it went better still, with unexpected developments, culminating in a record scene that lasted three solid hours, finishing up at 12 p.m. *Most* thrilling, but I'm rather horrified at Tony.

*Saturday
June 22*

That morning we both felt very cheap—reduced from sixpence three-farthings to all-in-this-box-one-penny. It was partly fatigue, but in great measure it was emotion. However, **it does R. more good than anything, because it helps her forget for a space!** . . . Strayed in Erasmus' walk, and sat in John's grounds eating raspberries, but a pound of them does go a long way . . .

It was a most deliciously hot day. *Really* hot.

CAMBRIDGE — LONDON (JERMYN ST.)

*Sunday
June 23*

Another hot day. We didn't get up till 1, but played in Ruth's room and got Tony "up against it". Afterwards we packed hastily and acted again. Then, alas, we had to leave . . . In the evening I was obsessed by Tony and it was hard to settle down.

The poppies in the fields were just wonderful—a narrow scarlet tide.

*Tuesday
June 25*

R. came with the letters. **It's awfully complicated and pathetic, the family were quite sure she'd broken it off** . . . That evening I was most hatefully tired, but I wrote six letters, and really one good day at them would clear the decks. I must try —

On June 29 Dorothea was joined by Babs. They motored to Ringwood in the New Forest where they spent a few days. On her return to London Dorothea bought "stays with about two bones in them" and began work on Outlaw's Luck, *a novel about her play-character Kid Prevost.*

JERMYN ST. — WINCHESTER

Thursday
July 4

Called for Pearl and Ruth and went off, leaving Dad. I do wish he were coming too . . . Winchester is very beautiful, and we stayed at the God Begot Inn. 15th century—delightful rooms, all named King Alfred, Empress Matilda and so on (and Hygeia and the Druid's Well). But sad to say, there was an Ella Wheeler Wilcox* poem in every room. When R. and I got to our attic (which felt like a church porch), there was one there, and I tore it down and concealed it under the dressing table, and forgot to replace it when we left next day . . .

SALISBURY — EXETER

Saturday
July 6

Acted in the morning. Went on to Exeter. The Devon lanes are very deep, you can't see out of them at all, and the banks are grown with tall nodding foxgloves and the hedges are hung with honeysuckle. Such great sweet branches of it! . . . The Cathedral is wonderful, black and rich and broad . . . But I was tired and went to bed soon—such a huge bed, by the way! and we acted a little in the evening, and ate raspberries and Devonshire cream . . .

EXETER — PLYMOUTH

Monday
July 8

Got up late and crawled around the Cathedral . . . Then we went to Plymouth. Another wet cold day, else it would have been a prettier journey. But I always love motoring, even in the rain. On arriving I promptly went to bed. We none of us were to sleep much that night, for the rooms were light as day and the town unbelievably noisy . . .

PLYMOUTH — PENZANCE

Tuesday
July 9

Still wet. Left for Truro, where we got our letters and saw the modern cathedral, which is correct and cold. We lunched at the 17th century Red Lion, *ô jour funeste*! Reached Penzance to find the sea all grey and stormy, and myself

Ella Wheeler Wilcox: Writer of poetic homilies, including "Laugh and the world laughs with you/Weep and you weep alone".

OPPOSITE: *Spring in Sussex* Tom Roberts

in a fever to act . . . but R. and Mother and Pearl were all ill that night and most of that day. The Red Lion pie, which I hardly touched. Poor dears —

GLASTONBURY — WELLS

. . . We went to Wells in the afternoon. It was very hot and the hedges were white with dust . . . The Cathedral is splendid, but they won't let you in on Sundays, no how, and the Close has notices up that say that children are not allowed to play, shout, run about or make any noise whatever. R. wanted to write "For of Such is the Kingdom of Heaven" underneath in white chalk . . .

WELLS — BATH — GLOUCESTER

The morning was stifling hot. We prowled about and went on to Bath, where we liked the 18th century place and the Abbey. The Roman remains didn't thrill me, but they *are* interesting. Beau Nash rather crowded them away . . .

I think it was in the cloister of the Wells Cathedral that there was an epitaph to a lady "whose Domestick and Conjugal Virtues were the comfort of her Husband". Most improper *I* think.

Reached Gloucester in the evening. Such a different sort of place—manufacturing, one would think. Quite noisy people, and great thrill about a circus. R. wanted to go out with P. and me in an evening dress, but we wouldn't let her . . .

GLOUCESTER — HEREFORD

The cloisters of the Cathedral at Gloucester have very rich fan vaulting, and they are wonderfully preserved. The *lavatorium* at one side, and the place where the monks used to keep the towels—as M. said, one would rather play in it—are the only ones I have seen . . . I think it was here that we found the tomb of Waller's wife—very charming:

"In graces Great, in stature small,
As full of Spirits as voyd of Gall."

— with Waller, raised on one elbow, looking at her. But he's buried in London, alas. And another epitaph which ended:

> " 'tis thus disconsolate a widow sings.
> T.P. her cousin hopes for better things."

... R. and I made daisy chains in the churchyard and gave them to one of the forgotten graves. We went to Hereford by way of Chepstow and Tintern in the afternoon, all along the Severn and the Wye Valley.

The poppies are still in the fields, and the grass is beginning to yellow. We reached Hereford in time for dinner, and put up at the Green Dragon. The Cathedral is fine, and has a wonderful sculptured font. We greatly loved William the Conqueror—like an aggressive washerwoman.

Following a day apiece in Hereford and Oxford, the party returned to London.

... All very much depressed at the end of the tour. Spent the evening neck-deep in letters and found I had missed two engagements.

Saturday July 20

Dad and I motored down to Greenhithe for the prize-giving for officer cadets on the *Worcester* ... Joseph Conrad and Perceval Gibbon [Conrad's close friend] were waiting for us, the latter in a peculiarly impish mood. It was a hot, glaring day. The Capt. and his neurasthenic Italo-Irish wife were awfully kind. The ship is interesting. She is 80 years old and very like what Nelson's ships must have been. And the boys are dears, so straight and clean and manly. There was a crowd, but we were distinguished visitors up on the platform.

We saw them man the yards—a ceremony extinct everywhere else—and heard Sir Thomas Sutherland's tiresome Methodistical speech and old Lord Brassey's rather nice one, and various others. The prizes were nice—sextants and aneroids and telescopes and naval books, and the last one was Conrad's *Mirror of the Sea.*

Friday July 26

Gibbon and I talked of magic and snakes and Russian realists and other things, and he tormented me about the *LBD*, but please the pigs he'll forget to review it! He's very amusing —and rather cruel . . .

Whilst Dorothea was touring the English countryside, Sir Charles was, in accordance with Lord Chelmsford's commission, "studying the treatment of delinquent and neglected children in Great Britain". Between July 24 and 30 he was, as well, an observer at the First International Eugenics Congress held at London University. The eugenic ideal was the "well-born child, resulting from strong germ-plasm" (from the Congress Report).

The Congress considered how geniuses of the order of Bach and Mozart were made and cautiously discussed the ethics of sterilisation of criminals, the sub-normal, "drug-fiends" and epileptics, among others. The Titanic *had sunk only three months earlier. With the cry, "Women and children first!" fresh in their minds, some eugenists questioned whether "the strong men on the* Titanic *were not making a mistake . . . in giving way not only to their own wives and children, but to the women and children in the steerage". One speaker answered that "the primary need of society was . . . for men able to conduct its affairs; if so, these men made a mistake".*

Monday July 29

. . . Went to the Eugenics Congress with Dad and heard an interesting debate on Eugenics and Militarism. Prof. Kellogg read a paper . . . and then Prof. Loria read a paper on the Psycho-Physiological Elite, in a Can-ze-Ethiopian changzispo? English that was killingly funny . . .

Tuesday July 30

. . . Exhibition of modern etchings and Kay Nielson's black and white drawings at the Dowdeswell Galleries . . . Of course, he is generally morbid and Beardsley—using that as an adjective—but his design is marvellous, and his imagination, and his delicacy of line — I hesitated and was lost. It was extravagant, too, for all the best were sold—

the illustrations to *The Book of Death*—such a terrified Pierrot, such a helpless white Columbine, and *such* a sweeping, inexorable Death! . . . I got *Adoration*. It has not the delicacy of his other work, but it is very strong. He's only 26, they say—and I'm sure his work is going up in price, so I had to buy now! Babs came in the evening and we talked, mostly of her Creighton-Webb [Babs' fiancé, a naval aide-de-camp]. **I was dying to write.**

Early in August Dorothea spoke to her parents about staying on in London after their return to Australia. It would be the first time that she had lived away from home. Sir Charles and Lady Mackellar could scarcely refuse permission—Dorothea was, after all, 27 years old. Nervous at the thought of leaving her in London, even though she would have Ruth for company, and concerned for her welfare during the return journey to Australia, they wrote to Eric, suggesting that he should make immediate plans to come to England. Dorothea eventually heard from Eric at the end of September. Though he was none too happy about it, he agreed to be in London by April the following year. Meanwhile Dorothea started looking for a flat.

. . . Decided about going away. Felt a worm.

Wednesday
August 7

. . . I went flat-hunting with Mr H. Malcolm and we had a deliriously amusing morning. The first char came out of Dickens, and I think the second did too. "Is this house to let?" "*Never!—Nothing*. God forbid that anyone else should live in a 'ouse like this. A 'orrid 'ole, and many's the lady and gent I've told so. Cellars underneath it, time o' Queen Hellizzebuth. Come down it? Bless yer 'eart, o' course y'can. I fell down it twicet. See me foot? (Waggling it) I've ben like that hever since. Funny, ain't it?—"

Friday
August 9

. . . The next was a "sort o' pretty little 'ouse—*but* may be to let—and I'm afraid I spoke sharp, but I'm like that. Many 'ave told me so. It's being used to 'avin' a lot o' servants hunder me—and you've got to speak sharp. Sharp but kind —" 14 Cheyne Row. A charming place with delightful furniture, but

we couldn't see the bedroom, because Mr De Bruce wasn't up, and that char "on'y came in tempery, and Miss 'Ayman was coming back from Germany tomorrow for lunch and might say if she wanted to let". On being interrogated, Mr De Bruce (who was dressin', would we like to see 'im?) admitted that he didn't know much about it because he'd only come in for the night. Miss 'Ayman let it from Miss Dawson-in-the-Profession, *You* know. A dear little house . . .

There was a loud explosion, and we hung out of the window to see four scarlet fire-engines and a swiftly gathering crowd. Two doors away—electric cable fused, manhole blown up. Presently the crowd divided and two policemen came running out with a man—23 they said he was afterwards—on a hand ambulance. Head swathed in bandages, eyes closed, blue-white face, and a line of scarlet at his mouth. I thought for a second, "How strange that his lips have kept their colour!" and then realized that it was blood, like the crimson at his neck. He died an hour later. Three others were badly hurt too. They stopped the fire . . .

Thursday
August 15

. . . Began to revise, as I had no more exercise-book. Three more chapters to write.

Sunday
August 18

LONDON — HARWICH

Wet day. Wrote a little *Outlaw's Luck.* R. came. Felt headachey and exceedingly disinclined for travel, acted Lutyens . . . Fur coat in train, and glad of it . . .

Wednesday
August 21

THE HAGUE

Congress.* Amusing. They have too many papers so they're limited to 25 minutes by a bell, and it's lovely to see them scurrying to get it all in, and their different

Friday
August 23

Congress: The 2nd International Moral Education Congress, convened by the Moral Education League, a British association founded in 1897, which in its original manifesto sought the introduction of "systematic non-theological, moral and civic instruction into all schools". The phrase "non-theological" generated controversy, and in 1909 it was dropped, and replaced by the words "and to make the formation of character the chief aim in education".

methods of attack are most instructive. Got letters from M. and Ruth and went mad on Lutyens—can't write a line 'cause I have acting fever so badly.

There were all sorts of great people speaking. It's interesting because there are two Rows on—Religious and Political—and all the Dutch Catholics are forbidden to attend. But there are R.C.s from every other country and the discussions are heated, every now and then. The Govt. are afraid of offending the R.C.s and so they suddenly withdrew all support, and that's why we're assembled in the Diergaarde (Zoo) instead of the Town Hall. But the Queen Mother and the Prince Consort are both patrons. How funny! . . .

BERLIN

Sunday August 25

Arrived 8 a.m., awfully tired, of course, and it was wet, but *that* didn't matter, and they thought we were a ménage that had quarrelled badly, because we refused one room, even for an hour. So they gave us two double rooms and I washed my hair with great success. In the afternoon we walked in the Tiergarten [Zoo] and called on the Rahts. What a dreary life! Constant "enjoyment". Very kind they are. So-o tired. Wrote a little because I couldn't help it, and went to bed and slept like a log for twelve hours . . .

Tuesday
August 27

Went to the Foreign Office and met Wirklicher Legationsrat Wedding, a lovable, nervous and very much overworked man, and his sub. Baron Reinbach, who reminds me a little of Capt. Scarlett, though physically they have nothing in common but a gentle expression, and this man's sensitive, handsome face is pulled out of shape on the left side by the inevitable great student-scars.

Wrote a little. Went to the Royal Theatre with the Rahts and saw *Der Groesser Koenig* . . . Play itself slow and patriotic. Incidental music by King Frederick the Great himself—charming 18th century stuff. I had no idea he composed like that! Supper afterwards at the Hotel Bristol with the Rahts—gorgeous, of course . . .

Wednesday
August 28

. . . The Waisenhaus [orphanage] is awfully interesting, especially the Hospital for babies, but *frightfully* sad. Because they are children from the poorest parts of Berlin. Germs of diphtheria —and of uglier things —I liked young Reinbach for being sorrier for the children than he was ashamed of the diseases with me. Badly said, but I can't stop to disentangle it . . . Wrote a little because I couldn't help it, but really I was too tired to do anything decent.

Out to Zeblendorf to a great institution there. It is magnificently done, and the children are given things of their own and put on their honour, and there are museums of cooking and sewing and shoemaking and so on. *Very* interesting—to show how things evolve, and the difference between good and bad material. Also we heard a very good little concert, but I got so tired that I fainted, to the disgust of the town clerk.

Luncheon in Dad's honour given by the Secretary of State, Kiderlen Waechter . . . Everybody was charming. The only other woman was Lady Granville . . . Afterwards I lay down, and then finished *Outlaw's Luck* in a fashion—I'll revise later . . .

. . . In the afternoon we went to say goodbye to the Rahts . . . and in the evening we went to the Command Night at the Opera. A very gorgeous affair, and we had the front seats in one of the royal boxes, and saw the imperial party awfully well. The Kaiser looks amazingly young and strong, though they say he's ill. The Empress much older. Prince Eitel is a great big thing, the only big one of the family. The little princess is rather sweet. The play was *Der Gr. Koenig* (I wish it had been another), and the officers did look nice, filling much more than half the theatre.

It was a funny feeling **to have such *heaps* of opera-glasses levelled at one, but I took kindly to it.** Besides, a Spanish crowd ought to harden one to that.

Supper afterwards at the Adler, another great hotel . . . *And* then Wedding had ordered my very own special cigarettes. I never knew such people for spoiling one (except perhaps in Q., **and then there were reasons**) . . .

Got up rather before 5.30 and went to the military parade with Dad, Wedding, and Frau and Frl. Matthieu by carriage . . . We were close behind the Emperor, a little bit to one side, and so we saw everybody marching their best . . . *Two* Army Corps—and it's the last that will ever be held on the Tempelhofer Feld, because it's wanted for building sites. And there were two dirigibles and ten 'planes in the air at the same time, which thrilled me. *So* cold! But fine, except for about three drops. The crowd was nice afterwards—the arriving was quite exciting, but now as I write, in great haste and very tired, it all seems like a cross between a child's dream and a cinematograph show . . . Dad has gone to the Kaiser's dinner with the fretful Col. Russell, and I ought to be packing now . . .

The next day Dorothea and her father journeyed to Copenhagen, where Sir Charles continued his inquiry into the treatment of delinquent and neglected children. On September 8 they returned to London, where Ruth was preparing to leave for Italy with her cousin Janet Stephen.

Monday
September 9

. . . Ruth came. We talked off some of our surplus and acted the Lutyens crowd all day. It went well, but my head was really bad and I could hardly see . . . I wish she wasn't going, for both our sakes, but it won't be so *very* long.

Old Lady Mansfield said to me . . . "I'm very fond of Tom, but some years ago, down in the country, what must he do but get mixed up with a farmer's daughter. I sent for her and said, 'My good girl, this is all nonsense, you know. He wants to marry you now, but you must see it would never do. I'll tell you what I'll do for you. I'll give you £300 and a bonnet shop.' So I got her a very nice little bonnet shop in Bath, very comfortable she was, and we sent Tom out to Mexico as an attaché. Well, while he was there the Portuguese Minister was changed. There was an interval of 14 days before the next one came out, and Tom had heard something, so he went over the cottage of the Legation, took plans of it, had one exactly like it run up on a plot of ground two miles away that he'd bought, and the Portuguese Envoy went into *that* while Tom tore down the other. There was a gold mine underneath that he'd heard about, you know. But of course he had to let the Government into the secret, and I always think they were most unfair, because they made £80,000 out of it, but Sir William said that Tom would have to resign: they couldn't have that sort of thing going on.

"And then came the war, and he went out, of course, and I'm blessed if that bonnet-shop girl didn't go out as a hospital nurse, and look after him when he was wounded, and marry him! They're in South Africa now—and I'm sure I hope they'll stay there."

. . . Drove with the parents to Battersea and Hyde Parks, began to make a
September rhyme . . .

Saturday
September 21

Another sunny day. Made the rhyme in the park . . .

Sunday
September 22

Whilst in Spain Dorothea had received her first copy of The Little Blue Devil.
*By August it was on sale in Australia priced at 3/6d. The reviews were good,
though one that she was sent caused her to comment: "Common enough to
make one squirm, but meant well, and very funny, especially where he speaks
of Father."*

"I don't know sweet Ruth," wrote "Gossip" of the *Stock and Station Journal,*

> "but I do know the gentle Dorothea, and when I read the book, I just laughed,
> right out, at the sheer devilry of it. Dorothea Mackellar is the daughter of Sir
> Charles Mackellar, and we all know him. Some of us love him and some of us
> don't, and he must have done a lot of good in his time to have made so many
> enemies. He is one of us, and his daughter has written some of the sweetest
> things that Australia has ever produced. When I saw that Dorothea and Ruth had
> collaborated in a book, 'sez I, to misilf I sez, sez I' there's going to be something
> sweet in this—an evening lullaby, a love story, a pathetic romance . . . Dorothea
> and Ruth: sweetly innocent creatures who have no idea of the tragic relations
> of life. Rats! Girls are deep! My word they are! Some of them who look as innocent
> as saints are deep as the sea, and the devil lies at the bottom. The story of *Little
> Blue Devil* is a ripping yarn, full of queer things, and pathos, and hard times
> and things you would never expect two girls to talk about, and 'damns' scattered
> all about the book as if it was written by an old bushman . . ."

Took O.L. to A. P. Watt,* but he was out. Left it and walked home, looking
at picture shops by the way . . . Washed hair and wrote heaps of letters—in
fact all there were to write—including one to Ruth; and talked a little to [cousin]
Clare. She *is* beautiful nowadays. Such a golden lady— as Hewlett would remark.
Rose-and-golden, especially in the evening, when she came to dinner in a frock
that matched her cheeks, trimmed with gold that was like her hair, and she
wore topazes in that hair and in her ears—I couldn't take my eyes from her . . .

Tuesday
September 24

. . . Left letter of introduction on Mrs John Lane* . . . In the evening we went

Wednesday
September 25

Watt: Alexander Watt, England's first literary agent.
Lane: Annie Lane, author of the American national hymn "To Thee, O Country".

to the Coliseum to see Bernhardt. She's rather pathetic now, poor dear . . . Also saw rather a good conjurer . . . and a brutal suffragette skit. I am glad to say that the audience (mainly masculine) applauded very little. The latter part of it quite upset the man behind me. He kept on murmuring, "Oh, poor devil. Oh, *stop* it, *stop* it —" I would like to have shaken his hand.

Thursday
September 26

. . . Walked along the Embankment and watched the river in the pearly mist that the sun was struggling through. An Embankment Artist did my Portrait— for a Penny, and it was as poor as he . . . Then motored (sounds so grand, that!) to Harrods for stockings. Drove with Mother in Regent's Park.

Saturday
September 28

Got gloves and discovered that the *Spectator* has printed the September rhyme . . . Afternoon: Went to show Dad the flat* (he approves) and then to the Zoo. There was a bitterly cold wind and most of the Australian animals there (including me) didn't like it . . .

Thursday
October 3

. . . *Very* cold. Wrote letters and got a reproachful—I may say reproving—one from Alston Rivers, because of using an agent. But they spoilt it by the last paragraph, so I'm not worrying as I otherwise should. Walked *hard*, but it was all I could do to keep warm.

Friday   October 4

Walked right along the Embankment and through Billingsgate, enjoying the queer names of the lanes. Huggin Lane, Three Cranes Lane (only there were a lot more when I saw it—joke), Beer St., Allhallows Lane, and so on . . . I wandered in the Tower Gardens. The grey towers looked very nice in the sunshine through a screen of autumn leaves, and the sad loafers on the benches blended in the picture. And some were young, too. Then I went home on top of a 'bus with three jolly Chinese women — and two of 'em were small-foot ladies, what's more. Odd!

In the afternoon Mother and I went to Bunhill Fields and saw Bunyan's tomb and the Cromwells, and Susanna Wesley's, and the unfortunate Mistress

flat: Dorothea had found a flat in Douglas Mansions, Cromwell Road, South Kensington. She planned to move into it with Ruth at the end of the year.

OPPOSITE: *The Green House, St John's Wood*   Robert Bevan

Mary Page, who was Tapd [tapped] 66 Tymes in 67 Months and 240 Gallons were taken from Her without Ever Repining or Fearing at the Operation, and Isaac Watts. "Oh Gord our 'Elp in Ages Past" and many others . . . We came home by the Embankment through a thick salmon pink mist (rather like Jules' restaurant's *purée d'écrevisses*) and a bloodred sun was reflected in the water by Westminster Bridge . . .

Tuesday
October 8

Went to the 2nd Post-Impressionist exhibition,* at the Grafton Galleries. Weird and interesting. I liked some of Matisse, especially his *Pose du Nu* and his *Danseuses*; though they look like starfishes and badly filled bolsters, they *are* dancing . . . I liked some of the Russian things too. They were strange and stirring, but the Cubists seemed unsuccessful and *why* are all one's sensations supposed to be blackish-grey? Mine aren't. The only criticism of *La Femme au Pot de Moutarde* that seemed at all adequate was that of an old gentleman who gasped, "My God!" and fled. Gauguin's rather nice. The sculpture seems mainly decadent Egyptian in style . . .

Monday
October 14

. . . A pile of letters, and Conrad's last book with an inscription—he *is* a dear . . .
Mother and I are both feeling that it is time we were away, exciting as London is at present. We hate to move, but it will be all right as soon as we are going.

Tuesday
October 15

. . . Watt says Alston Rivers' terms are Rot. So when he has heard from Mr Bean (another week's delay—Blow) he's going to propose other terms, which they won't take but Mills & Boon will. *Bueno—*
Westminster Gazette has taken "Flower and Thorn" . . .

Saturday
October 19

. . . Beautiful sunny morning. Sat in Hyde Park by a bed of faint mauve asters. The mist is very thick among the trees, but the sun does shine . . . Wrote to Ruth, who is in Venice by now, I suppose.

Wednesday
October 23

Saw exhibition of Phil May, Clausen and Rackham at Leicester Galleries. The Phil Mays and Rs very clever. I loved R's illustrations to *Aesop's Fables*—I wanted to buy lots. (But didn't.) But the Clausens are just *Beautiful*—all of them, and they're so different. London things and Country things . . .

exhibition: The exhibition also included works by Cezanne, Picasso, Braque and Bonnard.

... Wrote letters, signed Douglas Mansions lease. (Dad scared them by being terse and flopping things about, just for the moral effect.) ... Princess Despina Karadja was here when I got back, and she and Dad were getting on like a house afire ...

Thursday
October 24

Felt ill—and things are beginning to rush.

Calls. Harry Lauder in the evening. Yes, the other turns were very good, but he overshadows everything. What a personality! You can't help liking him— and after all his comic songs he sang *Annie Laurie* most divinely, and I nearly cried ...

Friday
October 25

Goodbye calls, and everybody was very sweet to us. There *are* a lot of nice people in the world.

Sunday
October 27

More goodbyes and packing . . . Depressed.

Monday
October 28

Dorothea and her parents left London on October 31 for two weeks in Paris, but the planned diversions failed to captivate, and she turned to translating a number of German poems. Sir Charles and Lady Mackellar were, in effect, already on their way home to Australia. Dorothea travelled with them as far as Rome, where she met up with her cousin Pearl and, on November 27, with Ruth and Ruth's cousin Janet.

ROME

... It was a cold bright morning. We threw our pennies into the Fountain of Trevi and saw the Capitol once more, and the little Temple of Vesta ... And Santa Maria in Cosmedin, which is certainly one of the nicest churches in Rome— not Renaissance at all—and so well restored, queer and Byzantine. And we drove up on the Pincio, but that was in the afternoon. Then Ruth came, and the wrench. We all hated it, but were sensible. I think Father felt it most of all. It got very cold. They drove away in the dark and I hurried off and talked hard. Ruth's a dear.

Thursday
November 28

Dad's birthday. He's at Port Said. The others went out early and I followed

Thursday
December 5

them to the Palazzo Doria, where we saw the wonderful Velazquez *Pope* and some good Brueghels . . . The fever for buying has come on me since I saw the girls' things. Pretty leather trinkets, if you can call them so—and so on.

Went out quite early—for us—and drove about saying goodbyes to all the lovely places. Very sad at leaving . . . Then we shopped and I bought a Golden Crown (Mother's gift) and lots of other things. There was an exhilarating feeling in the air. Tea with R. and Pearl in the Piazza di Spagna, and called at the Marchesa de Viti's in the black beautiful dark, and more shopping (for R.), and a conversation with an old ruffian on Art and Anarchy and various Social Questions—started by my furs. Then home to pack till I nearly dropped.

Monday
December 9

MILAN — PARIS

An early start but no rush. That was lucky, as we had none of us slept much. Crossing the Alps, the snow was too glorious for words. Deep and dazzling (there was snow even by Lake Maggiore) and all the waterfalls were frozen, shining icicles. We went over/thro' the Simplon, and through Switzerland all day. I never saw so much snow before. The forests came straight out of Russian fairy tales, loaded with cotton-wool they were, and it was a foot deep everywhere, and sometimes drifted *ever* so high. Lausanne was rather nice, but it began to get dark . . . and a tiresome old Frenchwoman insisted that the windows must be closed, so we nearly fainted several times. It was a relief to find that Paris was quite warm . . .

Thursday
December 12

Stayed in bed quite late and found the pale sunshine pouring into my window in the mansard-roof—it's worthwhile climbing five or six flights for that! Washed hair slowly and tidied a few things. It took the whole morning . . .

Friday
December 13

Same as yesterday—lots of letters, including one from A. P. Watt to say that Mills & Boon had taken *OL* "on *our* terms"! Hurrah . . .

Saturday
December 14

I always mean to write in the mornings, but I wake so late and tidying takes all the time. Shopped for shoes. Pinet *fantaisies*—all peacock-blue and gold . . . Comedie Francaise in the evening . . . *Bagatelle* . . . a thin thing really.

Monday
December 16

OPPOSITE: *In a Paris Studio* Agnes Goodsir

Ruth came in the morning with a bunch of violets and we did Rags and Remington, which is beginning, alas, to obsess me in a delightful but *very* uncomfortable manner . . .

PARIS — LE HAVRE

Packing in the morning, shopping in the afternoon, and an awful two hours at the Bercy Douane (on account of the laurel diadem), which reduced me to tears of sheer exhaustion. Ruth and Janet—train and Rouen very lovely in the clear dark—and a very comfortable steamer with a cushiony, pleasant stewardess. Wrote Remington thoughts in the train.

Saturday December 21

Arrived in the blackest night. I liked gliding up Southampton Harbour like that. It stirred all sorts of sleeping memories. A polite Customs man—and long, long waits on the railway station—Oh, what does it matter?

Christmas Day

A nice quiet friendly one in pouring rain . . .

REMBRANDT HOTEL — DOUGLAS MANSIONS

Tuesday December 31

Packed, shopped hard and joyously at Harrods for all manner of household things, including some lovely little flowering azaleas in pots. Hardly dared to breathe for thinking what the afternoon would be like. Went to the flat, which looks very comfortable, and proceeded to unpack and straighten things till Ruth came. Talked, breathless with excitement—forgot we were tired and acted—but I forget what!

*Wednesday
January 1 1913*

Our breakfast is very nice and private and we dress partly, or altogether, if we feel energetic enough. I wasn't, very, so I stayed in and read a little of Pepys and wrote home letters.

... Little walk, household things. This quiet life ought to be good for us.

Friday
January 3

A thick white fog, so that we could hear the motor lorries passing underneath us as we stared down on the cloud, and yet we saw nothing—*nothing*. *Peter Pan* in the evening . . . . A nice supper at home.

Monday
January 13

... Captain Gordon came in the afternoon and was a dear, but he told me Mac had been hurt in the reaper-and-binder—and Eric had a much worse smash than I'd ever known at polo— . . .

Friday
January 17

Arranged book of verses and christened it *The Witch-Maid*. Went for a wet walk by my wild lone and made a rhyme for Savill* . . .

Tuesday
January 21

Lay long in bed—**acting Winifred and Tony**. Did rows in the Savill household . . . Supped at the Campbell's—amusing and very nice. Savill in a bad black mood. Acted rather a good scene on coming home—Jenny and Pat and he. We do get our change out of these people.

Sunday
January 26

... Mr Gordon Bedford* and Mr Emerson came in the afternoon and stayed a good while. Rather nice things, both lonely. A pity one can't be as kind to people as one wants to . . .

Wednesday
February 12

Shopped at Liberty's—Oh the fascinating place!—and the Army and Navy Stores. In the evening dined with Mr Emerson and went with him to *The Importance of Being Earnest*, which was good, and I enjoyed the whole thing, though dreadfully tired.

Monday
February 24

Went to Mr Grimsdale, who is a nice one. He examined my eyes, and I have slight astigmatism. I came home very blind indeed and in the afternoon we went to *The Piper* (F. R. Benson's Company). It's a sweet play and he is very good except when he rants. The children were the nicest things there. Preceded by *The King's Minstrel*—ab-so-lutely Rotten.

Wednesday
February 26

Savill: Dorothea and Ruth created new play-characters during their stay in England: Mr Savill and Jenny, Winifred, Pat, Lutyens, Ripon, Myers and Madeleine, Glynde and his faithful hound, Margarita and Wynyard, Francesco de Paoli, Petronella, the Lawlesses, and many others.
Gordon Bedford: Ruth's father.

Blind. R. had to open my letters! Did Tony being skidded on by Ripon's motor and Savill with gunpowder in his eyes. Afernoon: We paid heaps of calls and Mr Gordon Bedford came to tea and stayed till dinner, to which we did not ask him, in spite of his lonely eyes, for R. wasn't at all well. *Did* act a little of the Savills, however.

Saturday   March 1

. . . In the afternoon we went to *Nell Gwynne, The King's Favourite*, at the Lyceum (because R.'s friend Miss Tittell Brune was in it). I *never* saw such a melodrama. The gallery hissed and roared like steam escaping, and the King and his courtiers talked mixed modern slang and tushery. The worst of it was the length, 3 hrs. 35 minutes. We were pulp at the finish . . .

Tuesday   March 4

. . . Wrote a note or two, and in the afternoon Miss Brune came— and she is just as sweet and fascinating as R. always said. She would be so easy to make love to—I nearly did, lots of times. And R. told her about our plays, and she was very thrilled and quite understood, and she is going to play with us! It will be fun to have a real actress in them.

In the evening we went to the Russian ballet at Covent Garden. They did an exquisite thing called *Narcisse*—Nijinsky is marvellous, and Piltz as the most adorable Bacchante was like a figure from a Greek vase come to life. Karsavina was wonderful as Echo. Then *l'Oiseau de Feu*, a beautiful fairy-tale, and *Carnaval* (Schumann's music so beautiful too). We loved the queer shy woodland things in *Narcisse*. They were so daring and timid. And the little Enchanted Princesses in *l'Oiseau de Feu*.

Quite suddenly Dorothea mentions that she and Ruth are planning a second co-written novel based on their play-characters. The plot concerns an Australian mining engineer, Remington, who rescues a boy named Rags from the clutches of a crazed Chinaman. Rags and Remington enjoy life together. Then Viola enters upon the scene . . . The new book is given the working title Remington's

Boy, though this will later be changed to Two's Company.

Worked a little, stuck fast in a story—I shall have to leave it till Eric comes.
Wrote a few letters and began to discuss the division of labour in Remington's
Boy . . . Afterwards we went to the dear Despina's, where there was also a Swedish
damsel who said, "I have been marrying my sister, just." Went for a walk in
the Park, still talking about R's B, and then to call on Mrs Campbell. The maid
said wistfully, "No, she's not in—at *all*" . . . Milnes Stephen came to dinner.
We stayed up very late because R. and I were still wanting to discuss the book.

Foggy and raining in the beginning. Boat Race Day . . . Went to Miss Brune's
with Ruth shortly after lunch . . . She has a flat overlooking the River at
Hammersmith and thousands were flocking to Hammersmith Bridge to watch
the boats pass. It was a nice party . . . Miss Brune flopped us straight into the
middle of her new play with us. By and by when she takes it more seriously
(as she probably will), it ought to be really good . . .

It was all interesting, and the crews shot under the bridge with Cambridge
leading by lengths—not a soul of those thousands was allowed on the bridge,
and it was strongly guarded by police, because the suffragettes had threatened
things. (More by token, when you go into a museum or gallery now, they
make you give up even your small purse-bags.) And by and by the Cambridge
flag went down and the crowd began to melt, and those nice *different* people
talked—and then we walked home to Kensington High Street because the crowds
were so great. In the evening we went to the Philharmonic Concert conducted
by Safonoff and heard a Symphony by Scriabin and Beethoven's *Choral
Symphony*—both very good and very well done.

Went to an exhibition of Manning's country pictures and Herbert
Draper's studies for pictures. Very nice. I wanted some of Draper's lithe
ladies, and lots of Manning's sunny sketches of horses and wind
and openness . . . Then to Ethel Gabain's exhibition of
lithographs and etchings. They're awfully good, and I
want to get several . . . but I don't like her use of colour
and so I don't think I shall get her to do me.

Both tired, too tired to begin Remington's Boy. In the evening we acted a dream or two, as it wasn't an acting day. It was fun.

Tuesday March 18

. . . Janet came to tea and we all went out to Holborn to hear Hewlett* read from *Helen Redeemed* and other things. Through those queer back streets into an unfinished, crowded, dark little raftery room where Hewlett (who has a fierce cat-face) read remarkably well, and it was good stuff, some of it. We liked his unaffected, business-like manner between whiles. I think I liked the last thing better than *Helen Redeemed* or *The Voyage* (which was good in patches, but aimless.) It was about a satyr and a scarf. After that we hurried to S. Paul's through a glorious blue night, very cold, and heard Bach's *Passion* music . . . Home on top of a bus till Ruth nearly froze—such a nice night—and cold supper and cigarettes and excitement and longings to be at work again. *Such* a good day.

Saturday March 29

. . . Tailor. He *is* a funny little man. "You gannot haf smoll bottons on zee skairt. Eet ees eempossible." . . . Went to see the dear Meg, who has just arrived Home, and Mr Patrick Chalmers* turned up, a small, very young, sandy Scotchman, quite unaffected, and inclining to be casual through nervousness. I liked him, and we showed him Masefield's *Ballads* and he loved them unashamedly. A little acting after dinner, but we were too tired really—and to bed.

DOUGLAS M. — COAKSBURY FARM [Derbyshire]

Wednesday April 9

Finish of packing—tips and excitement. A good journey. Tea at the delightful old Peacock Inn at Rowsley. Drive to Youlgreave. The Farm was built in 1726. It's exquisitely clean and fresh inside, and the scenery is lovely, though wintry as yet. Just a few primroses are peeping out.

Hewlett: Maurice Hewlett, novelist, essayist and poet.
Patrick Chalmers: In her old age, Dorothea liked to tell people that she had been engaged to be married to Patrick Chalmers. See also Introduction.

Got *Outlaw's Luck* in the morning. It began snowing at 8.30 in the morning and kept on all day. Soon everything was white and by night it was four inches deep. The trees looked so lovely and only the peacock was discouraged. Walked into Youlgreave through the snow, and snowballed each other coming back . . .

Friday
April 11

Got the first press notices of OL—*Times* and *Scotsman*. Good. Walked up the lane, a lovely soft windy April day, and did the Remingtons, who are always pleasant, and found seven new birds' nests, for the blackbirds and thrushes were very busy. In the afternoon, walking into Youlgreave, we found two more— one with three green eggs in it—but I fear the boys have found it too. In Youlgreave we went the prettier little walk down the river, all climbing and sunny and shining and new green leaves. "The primroses'll be coomin' oopth' dale", as Miss Dale said. Wrote a little.

Wednesday
April 16

Walked up the lane and found more nests. (One has *four* green eggs now, instead of three) and in the afternoon wrote a little more . . .

Friday
April 18

Walked along the dale and met two very nice children with their hands full of violets and primroses, and they gave them to us and showed us where they grew.

Sunday
April 20

A cable came, saying that Freda [Ruth's sister] was sailing by the *Malwa*. Great excitement. My mail full of accidents and illness . . . Walked to Bakewell in the afternoon and bought a crab, Macaulay's *Lays*, epsom salts, skirt binding, a whiting, entrance to chapel, chocolate cake, a writing block and a newspaper and galoshes—all for 4/3½d, mainly in coppers . . .

Tuesday
April 22

. . . Walked to Youlgreave and found that the dear nest had been robbed. Acted again (shipwreck).

Wednesday
April 23

Went marketing with a basket, and brought home the meat, and two ha'penny bunches of radishes that we bought from a man in the street. Walked a pretty walk, thro' the village, over the river and back, and my skirt split! . . .

Friday
April 25

The mail arrived, and Eric's letters, and he's coming on Friday! Three days earlier than I thought he could. I got so excited that I couldn't work all day. Also there arrived reviews—one *much* too long one from the *Spectator* . . .

Monday
April 28

Heaps of letters for us both from editors and publishers and authors and such, and Alston Rivers *have* modified their terms for Ruth. I'm so glad. Sat in the fields and wrote. Walked up the lane and found a nest-full of eggs. Did Savills.

COAKSBURY — DOUGLAS MANSIONS

Thursday
May 1

R. packed for me and got bluebells. Left sorrowfully and went by the forgetmenot path to Rowsley. Not a bad journey, and everything very cheerful at the flat . . . I went to bed.

Friday
May 2

Eric came. Got up in time to go to the station. R. came too, and the train was an hour late. We said the whole of Horatius while waiting. Then he came, and he looks very well—and we went home together, and yarned, and he stayed to dinner that night, and the dear Ruth went out on purpose, and he yarned more —**of the things that count** —and I was awfully excited.

Tuesday
May 6

. . . "Pat" [Patrick Chalmers] came and amused us as usual. "It's next week that you begin to sponge on your friends, isn't it? What night will you dine with *me?*" Dinner at the Rembrandt with Eric . . . and supper . . . at the Savoy. "Expensive women and expending men surrounding us — "

Two days later Dorothea and Ruth left Douglas Mansions. Dorothea moved into the Rembrandt Hotel, where Eric was staying. Most probably, Ruth moved into a nearby apartment, where she was shortly joined by her sister Freda.

DOUGLAS MANSIONS — REMBRANDT

Thursday
May 8

Cleared up and paid the last tip, and Eric came and went, and then we acted. It was a good thing that we chanced to have the Petronella play to finish up with. It took off the edge. Came with R. to the Rembrandt. That night talked to Eric . . . and I couldn't sleep for excitement at seeing him, and other reasons—partly lack of my usual hot milk!

Friday
May 9

. . . Pavlova with Eric in the evening. A very good programme at the Palace. She

did Liszt's *Rhapsodies* and Chopin's *Préludes* and some of the older things, and all the other turns were good.

Saturday
May 10

. . . The people at this hotel can't make us out. We talk to each other too hard.

Thursday
May 15

. . . Went out with Ruth in the morning to get fencing clothes at Harrod's, and in the afternoon to a private view of "Alastair's" pictures at the Dowdeswell Galleries. Devilishly clever and morbid, but I had to get one (the least fantastic) partly because I desired it and partly because I'm a weak fool and the proprietor showed us round! Wicked extravagance which was to worry me later . . . Oh, and Ruth showed me Enid Derham's* poems, and they're miles beyond anything *I* could do. I'm glad for Australian poetry—of course—but I'm sorry for me.

Friday   May 16

Had first fencing lesson in a nice *salle d'armes* [fencing studio] in Brompton Rd . . . Wrote diary and letters. Head ached (I wrote to Enid Derham).

Tuesday
May 27

. . . Bought opera cloaks with Ruth and was drunk with colour—the place being Liberty's . . .

Wednesday
June 4

Eric went to the Derby . . . A suffragette ran on the course and seized the bridle of the King's horse and was rolled over—she and the jockey both hurt. An awful thing, but the suffrage societies repudiate her. I suppose, though, that if she dies they'll make her a martyr. Poor thing—mad, of course.

Friday
June 6

Ordered coat and skirt at Bradleys. When you come out, an imposing person in uniform hurries up and asks permission to call your car, which you deny, but graciously, and proceed to mount a penny 'bus with your well-known elegance.

On June 14 Dorothea left London to visit friends and see the sights in Oxford, Cambridge and Chester. She returned to London in time for her birthday.

Derham's: Enid Derham, Melbourne-born poet and academic.

A nice hot day, but I felt ill and irritable and most abnormally depressed. Ruth came and brought me sweet presents, and we acted a little, and a cable came from Mother and Father and Mac—but nothing went well . . . I *never* had such nerves before. Walked with R. to Mrs Bradshaw's, and then bought a pretty hummingbird dress together as a sort of consolation.

Still felt ill. Lunch with Ruth and Mr Chalmers. Horribly depressed . . .

After I had finished writing a long mail (feeling worse than ever), Eric came in with Mr Dick Binnie. He said I looked white. There was some discussion and the upshot of it was that we went off to Sir Watson Cheyne in Harley St. (*vide all* the London novels) after lunch, and I was ordered to bed at once under suspicion of appendicitis. So I couldn't go to hear W. B. Yeats read his own poems at the Poetry Book Shop—and neither did poor Ruth.

REMBRANDT — 3 DEVONSHIRE TERRACE [Private Hospital]

Supervised packing and felt rather dazed, and in the evening drove with Eric and Ruth, feeling rather chilly about the heart, to a gloomy-looking brown brick box, a section of which I was to inhabit. But at any rate you can see a tree out of the window, and the last patient had thoughtfully left me her jar of great pink roses—and the dearest little bright-eyed nurse came in. I hoped at once that she was to be mine.

After Sir W. had examined me I saw him look at the matron and I knew what that meant, but they thought I didn't know. Eric was wiser. Wrote letters and thought.

Operation over early, and much pleasanter than the last time, owing to a wonderful drug called Scapolomin—but I can't spell it. Drowsed and existed through the day.

. . . Pain not nearly so bad as last time, didn't want visitors though, and people were awfully good about sending flowers—sheaves of white lilies, and great pink carnations, and roses. My little room was quite full.

Eric and Ruth came every day and I don't know what it would be like without

them. They are both so understanding. R. brings me books from the library, but nothing seems to grip much. Lady McCormick came, and Mrs Wesche, both very sweet. **I wanted my Mummy too!**

More visitors, carefully shepherded, and lots of jigsaw puzzles, and good talk from the Matron, yarns about St. Thomas' Hospital. Left on Friday, feeling limp.

Tuesday–Friday
July 29–August 1

REMBRANDT

Ruth's birthday and no chance of getting a present for her. Nightmare time at the hotel and frantic efforts to hurry the people who were making my surgical stays. Eric succeeded in time. Crowds and oppressed feeling.

Saturday–Friday
August 2–8

With Eric and Ruth for company, Dorothea convalesced at Chipping Campden in the Cotswolds. From time to time her heart "hurt abominably" and "wobbled". When she was pronounced well enough, they explored the countryside—"the fields yellow with harvest and the green orchards bright with apples and red plums". At other times Ruth and Dorothea would "lie in the garden, which was mainly bowling green, and watch the sky and the yellow-green fields, and the elms that grew up the lane between the blackberry hedges".

CHIPPING CAMPDEN — LONDON

Quite a successful journey, during which E. and R. behaved disgracefully— at least she says she didn't—and I wasn't much tired, only it *does* make me breathless, and I suppose I *mustn't* stay in London. Ruth ordered me lovely kimonos from Liberty's and I got two to console myself—a gold one and an old-red-lined brocade.

Tuesday
September 16

Went to the heart specialist, Dr H. D. Rolleston, a tall thin quiet man—I like him—and he says nothing is really wrong, but I must have absolute rest for *six weeks at the very least*. No theatre, no friends, no nuffin'. Recommended me to read the works of Balzac as an occupation. Ruth and I went to a consolation matinée in the afternoon—Masefield's *Nan* because it hurts me less to cry than to laugh . . .

Wednesday
September 17

OPPOSITE: *The Song in the Distance* Rupert Bunny

Miss "Beck" Cox came and she's going to Cornwall with me. I wish the doctors hadn't said Penzance when I want to go north, but *mafish — malaish —* . . . Mr Chalmers and Captain Rowe came to tea, but I was too breathless to talk to them . . .

LONDON — PENZANCE

Saturday   September 20

Awful scramble for train . . . and a breathless but not wholly unsatisfactory swinging southwards in the "Riviera Express"—what what! The Riviera Palace Hotel . . . is a country house turned into a hotel. The old part is charming and our rooms have magnolias and jasmine climbing round the windows, and the gardens are really beautiful, but I subsided immediately into bed and took no notice of anything.

Monday-Saturday   September 22-27

. . . Mainly soft grey rainy weather. The loveliest thing that happened was at four o'clock when the pilchard boats set out from Newlyn like a flock of grey gulls disappearing in the sea-mist—quite a hundred of them, grouping and scattering, smooth and silent as moonlight, and the most exciting thing was when Gustav Hamel, fresh from winning the Aerial Derby, came flying past my window with a rattling rush, and then away to sea . . . like a heron with the sunlight on its wings. **I live for the post.**

HOTEL RIVIERA — REGENT TERRACE

Happy returns to Mac. Moved and made a verse or two. I think I shall like our little lodgings. We have a view of the Bay and the sitting-room is inoffensive and cheerful. But *such* a talking landlady!

Warm, lovely day. Sat in the little green orchard and wrote letters, and walked a little on the Front, where the *noisettes* in Sunday best promenaded before the seated hats. Did a little 'broidery, and missed Ruth.

. . . Motored to Lamorna through a storm of sleet. The sea was rough jade-green and high-flung foam—all over the Front. Got fearfully excited and made a rhyme . . .

Couldn't sleep for breathlessness.

Lay on the shingly beach in the sun (the pebbles are granite and red and green serpentine—with bits of bottle glass hammered till it's rounded) and watched the red-sailed fishing boats go out from Newlyn one by one. Wrote lots of verse at night.

Thursday
October 9

Wild day, the foam dashed right over the Front, the gutters were running white with it and the whole broad road was brown with kelp. Too breathless to watch it long . . .

Friday
October 10

Still breathless, and therefore cross. Went (bath-chair) down to the beach, and the sea was smooth and violet-blue one day and rough grey-green the next.

Thursday–Friday
October 16–17

Rain. Wrote a jibbing chapter of Remington's Boy and did basket work.

Sunday
October 19

> *"White Paternoster, S. Peter's brother*
> *What have you i' the one hand? White book leaves.*
> *What have you i' the other hand? Heaven's gate keys.*
> *Open Heaven's gates, Streike Hell's gates*
> *And let every crysome child creep to its own mother —*
> *White Paternoster, Amen!"***

. . . . As I lay in the sunny bow-window, who should turn up but Eric? I *was* glad—and excited. Talked—and in the afternoon drove to St. Just, Morvah, Zennor, skirting the coast to Gurnard's Head. Wild moorland and grey rocks—mines, ghosts, bare-looking farms, and the sea. Squattering ducks, dying bracken and gold-sprinkled gorse.
    Very tired, but much happier.

Friday
October 24

Walked along the beach and played at being "cut off by the tide".

Sunday
October 26

PENZANCE — LONDON

The woods of Luxulyan, and all the others, were glorious gold and red as we came up in the train. Foamy yellow larches, and lacy curtains of lime, and gold sequins of the birches and such rich brown-yellow in the layered beech boughs.

Thursday
October 30

Amen!: From *Matthew and Mark and Luke and John* by Thomas Russell.

Friday *October 31*	Dr Rolleston was very well pleased with me, but says I must not stay in London . . .
Saturday *November 1*	. . . Eric went out in the evening and Pat came. He was very nice, sympathetic as ever, and we said poetry and told each other long stories in great content for some hours. He's rather a dear child.
Monday *November 3*	Tailor. Shoemaker. Ruth, with a very bad cold, poor darling. But oh, it was good to see her! She stayed hours too, and we sort of began to talk. Didn't get up to dinner, just read E. V. Lucas ("a bit of a nut [a dandy]—and does himself quite well", according to Pat) and made a translation or two.

Obeying Dr Rolleston's orders, Dorothea left London for Canterbury on November 14.

CANTERBURY — CAPEL HOUSE [Kent]

Monday *November 24*	. . . Mrs Conrad met me and told me rather amusing scandal about the Hunt-Hueffer* ménage, which wasn't allowed to come down to Capel House [the Conrad family home] that day—"They always mean Scenes, so I wrote and said the house was full." They were overly kind and hospitable and concerned, and Mr C. and I had a good talk, and after I went to bed Mrs C. came and talked and told me about her leg—poor brave woman* . . .

CAPEL HOUSE — LONDON

Tuesday *November 25*	. . . Met R. at Ashford, during a long dark lovely lonely journey to Charing Cross Station. Talked excitedly and played Jenny and Lawless in their Spanish train. (London all sparkling gold.) . . .

Dorothea's year of relative independence was nearly over. Soon she would return to her parents in Sydney.

Hunt-Hueffer: For many years Ford Madox Hueffer and Joseph Conrad had been close friends and had collaborated on several books, but by 1913, due to Hueffer leaving his wife and becoming embroiled in a scandalous relationship with Violet Hunt, he was no longer welcome at Capel House.
woman: Some time before, Jessie Conrad had torn the cartilages in her knees. One leg never healed, in spite of several operations, and she remained partially crippled for the rest of her life.

Did feel most awfully sick. I believe it was nervousness (sea and dentist), but it was certainly quite beyond my control. Most unpleasant. Wrote lots of farewell letters and a few lines of the last chapter of *Two's Company* [formerly Remington's Boy]. The day was bleak and blowy and wintry. The dentist is a kind one, and moreover the tooth didn't hurt me much, but it did take long. Then we did a scene of Savill's Daughter in the dentist's waiting room, because we were too early for Pat, and afterwards went through the winter dark to his office, which is a sumptuous big old place, all panelled, with a great stately stairway and Adam mantel-pieces, it appears, and two old dark portraits of a Guthrie and a Chalmers, the latter Pat's great grandfather. A very fine hook-nosed hawk-eyed old gentleman . . .

Monday
December 1

It was a nice tea, and Pat told some of his usual mixed stories—especially the one about the shipwrecked captain who didn't want the mate to blow out his brains because he liked that part best . . .

There is a beautiful view of St. Dunstan's Tower from P.R.C.'s window— it's just outside, and the tower was grey-silver and the sky dark sapphire, with black lacy bare boughs against it and the orange lights of a great building blinking in contrast.

Father's Birthday . . . Jim Fairfax brought me the MSS. of his two new books . . . He gave me a really beautiful poem on Segovia . . . He wants me to go to a Mrs Handcock to see if the voyage is propitious. But I haven't time!

Friday
December 5

Packing. Letters. Ruth and *The Wild Duck*. Very good—the audience wept heartily when Hedwig died, except me—so Ruth says I'm a hardhearted wretch . . . Eric came in like a whirlwind to say that the boxes have to be ready on Tuesday morning, ah me! —

Saturday
December 6

I forgot to say that I wrote the last words of the book on Friday night, but probably we shan't hear about it now till we're in Australia . . .

And here endeth this book, for I am sure more will happen on Monday than I can put into eight lines.

A World Torn in Two
1914–18

*Fragments of a 1914 diary exist. At first they show that little was changing
in Dorothea's life. She and Ruth returned to Australia and continued their
fantasy life in the midst of the usual round of shopping, lunches, dinners and
farewells. During a visit to Berrima, she wrote several poems. By June 9 she
was at Kurrumbede. Life in the country was mostly uneventful: some days
she struggled with depression, another day she "lay by the river and made a
baby fire, as big as my hand, and it burnt most beautifully, transparent gold
against the green of the clover". One day she met a Miss Wilkinson: "Attractive
poseuse, neutoric—***common and cheap*** . . . She offered me Lionel Lindsay
and that crowd, but as we don't know each other's address it probably will
come to nothing. Their ways may be curious, but they are an interesting lot,
and I believe in seeing what is going on in one's own town."*

*Since the assassination of Archduke Franz Ferdinand, heir to the Hapsburg
throne, on June 29, England had been moving steadily towards war. In the
weeks leading up to the start of the First World War, Dorothea seems not to
have considered the implications for Australia. Maybe the crisis in Europe seemed
remote. At first, even Austria-Hungary's declaration of war on Serbia fails to
rate a mention. She was more concerned with Ruth's birthday, with the proofs
of* The Witch-Maid *and the news that* Two's Company *had gone into its second
impression. She even reports the momentous announcement of August 2 with
a certain detachment.*

Went to Ruth for her birthday. At lunch a man rang Mr Bedford up to say
that Germany had declared war on Russia. Hope it's not true —It was only
on Thursday we had the news of Austria and Serbia, and it's affected things
so tremendously already —five firms in Sydney have failed in the last two days . . .

*Sunday
August 2*

*In the early afternoon of August 5, special editions of Melbourne newspapers
carried the news that Great Britain had declared war on Germany. Australia,
too, was now at war. Dorothea immediately responded by becoming a volunteer*

with the Red Cross, though she also had other things on her mind: on August 10 Ruth underwent an unspecified operation. Most of Dorothea's diary for the next three weeks is lost, but subsequent entries make it clear that Ruth made a good recovery. Soon the war was uppermost in her thoughts.

Saturday September 5

. . . I voted, and went to Ruth. In the same compartment as I were six soldiers (it's hard to get into an Elizabeth St. tram nowadays that isn't either loaded with khaki'd boys or with men going up to enlist). They were all well set up, and three out of the six were particularly goodlooking as well. Five of them were very young. One said abruptly, "I shall be glad when we get on board the ship." The eldest, a hardfaced, nice thing with a north of England accent—a non-com (the others were all Australians) said, "Yes, you'll be glad to get quit of your drill, won't you?" and they all laughed. Then one caught sight of a newspaper placard about the investment of Paris and observed cheerfully that "if these Germans only knew *we* was coming, they'd be clearing out". Another general laugh, and a remark from a boy with very long eyelashes and a peachlike brown complexion, to the effect that the news *would* demoralise 'em.

Non-com: Yeh—hardened fighting men of seventeen. The Infantry—in arms. That ought to scare 'em.

The very youngest *(laughing and flushing)*: Oh come on! Nineteen.

Non-com: I till y' they're coming down from the country—boys of sixteen and seventeen—I handled two yesterday. Big boys they were and they were cadets, they knew their drill. But they were two or three years under age.

2nd man: Then how could they get in?

The very youngest: *(off guard)* Y' don't have to show a birth certificate.

Non-com: *(like a flash) That* was lucky for *you*, wasn't it?

(**T.V.Y.** subsides)

3rd boy: Well, as long as they're strong, an' know the drill, I don't see why they shouldn't have the fun.

Non-com: Ah, but seventeen's too young. They shouldn't take them from their mammies at that age. It's cruel—

. . . Six brown hard, alert, cheerful things—it's an awful waste—and yet— . . .

. . . First letters from England about the War—one from Sir Richard Poore. They show what the papers wisely suppressed—that up to the last the Peace Party was clamouring for England to repudiate her treaty—saying "Why shouldn't we grow rich at their expense? Besides Germany means no harm—" I'm glad they failed—even counting the cost.

. . . First Aid examination at Heath. At first, during the bandaging, I was very nervous, but afterwards in the long wait I became quite placid and *I believe* I passed. Some of our class . . . are very good at this game. Others—for example:
Q. How would you treat a man suffering from shock?
A. I should fan him.

. . . In the afternoon I was to have gone to an Organ Recital with Mr Le Maistre, but on arrival at the Town Hall we found that it didn't recite, so we went to the Art Gallery and looked at some pictures and then sat on a rock in the Domain for a little time. The Harbour was very blue and bright, and Mother and Father came spinning by in the car and wouldn't look at us. So we walked home to tea. **Oh dear. It came out quite suddenly!** It's my unfortunate frankness—and his. **I didn't know what to say. For though of course I don't love him, it is just possible that I may some day and yet I don't want him to stay here getting hurt! In the end it seemed fairest to give him the chance he asked for!** I never did that before. I *am* sorry . . .

I slept very badly. To begin with they were singing in the streets till after 2 a.m. "*It's a Long Long Way to Tipperary*—" I could hear it in the distance. Soldiers, I think—and patrols collecting them. Far—near—far again—It was a beautiful moonlit night. And I had plenty to think about, beginning with the Growly Man of 14 years ago. And there were a good many **I liked better than this boy, and yet I had always been quite sure of myself before—** And my throat began to hurt, and my head ached and I don't **love him one bit.** If only I *did*, I wouldn't care a damn. It was nearly 4 when I finally got to sleep, and next moment (7.30) I was waked, with a raging headache that lasted all day . . .

Again, pages are missing. The diary resumes on October 22. Dorothea and Ruth are enjoying a little holiday away from Sydney.

Thursday
October 22

We went for a picnic. It was a most heavenly day, hot and still, and we went to the lost valley again and followed a great iguana who slid round a tree and showed us a rough path down to the house, near the straggling cannas and half-strangled sweet rose bushes. We went down to the creek and sat there all day, and I paddled and we did Ann-Tony at a picnic, and Jenny in S. America with Denzil and Conn. We sat on a mossy rock higher up and loved the shining, beautiful bush and the waratah trees and the baby creek that went over the silver sand so clearly, to join the big one that was muddled with flood-water still . . . We walked home a quite different way, along a beautiful smooth path that appeared suddenly, right along the gully by running streams and mossy rocks. It brought us out in the place where all the violets grow, quite near home, and there were pink and purple mists through the tall gold-green trees, and the sunset was glorious.

By November 12 they are home again.

Sunday
November 15

Hot and steamy. Lay on bed nearly all day reading Rose Macaulay's *Lee Shore*, which I like very much. **Mr Le Maistre came in the afternoon and stayed to supper.** Discussed what university we'd send our sons to, and what profession they'd be likely to choose— Dear me . . .

Tuesday
November 17

. . . Tried *hard* to get a black and red typewriter ribbon. You'd think that was simple enough? But no. Played with war maps and parents, and (very unwillingly) listened to an erotic conversation of great interest while struggling with the telephone.

Wednesday
November 18

Dentist and R., the former extremely agitating as it hurt beyond all reason. Shopping and a Patriotic Concert in the evening (for the Veterans' Home). Not at all bad. The Rally Round the Flag Boys numbers were alleviated in various ways, and some small children danced delightfully . . . And the veterans themselves were dears. I suppose it's really a more moving sight than regiments

of boys—but it's hard to choose. They were pleased and proud, anyhow, and I don't think they really felt pathetic at all, which was a comfort. Sat by General Harry Finn, bless him, and he told me what the ribbons and medals meant . . .

Friday
November 20

. . . Society of Artists with Ruth. Norman Lindsay's oils. He has only worked in that medium for 2 years, but has a large collection of small pictures—nudes, flesh very well done, with an extraordinary atmosphere of the late 16th Century or early 17th. I wanted some badly, but the two nicest were sold . . . His *Bacchanal* (oddly enough) tho' the drawing was good, was far, far too tame and stodgy. A nice governess-cart pony munching carrots, and the governess herself—pleasant girl—caressing it. She had discarded all garments except a lovely blue scarf, but was still a perfect lady . . .

The few surviving entries for December contain plans for a visit to Melbourne and reflect a growing friendship with George Le Maistre. By Christmas they are on first-name terms. Yet the war is never far from her mind: the final entry for the year records "A successful raid on Cuxhaven—3 hours, a good offset to the German baby-killing expedition to Scarborough—"

Sunday
January 3 1915

[PENNANT HILLS] It was a most beautiful blue and gold day, warm and fresh at the same time, and everything was looking its loveliest—and all the birds— the sort of day I thought, when I was very little, that they had in Heaven. It was the day appointed for a General Intercession because of the War. All the churches joined in it. We walked to the funny little wooden one at Thornleigh. It was crammed to overflowing—lots of men sat outside. I'm sure it had never been so full before. The old parson was quite excited and couldn't resist the opportunity of preaching an extra-long sermon . . .

Sunday
January 17

. . . In the afternoon went to the Milnes. Captain Twynam was there, just back from New Guinea. (Yesterday I met the contingent marching along L'pool St., very brown and hard as nails) . . . He told of Brian Pockley's death, and how a German soldier was just about to explode the mine in the road (a cylinder like those used for freezing meat, five feet long, filled with dynamite and quantities of nails) when one of our men saw the gesture and shot off his hand. Brian came up and amputated the remnant—immediately—chopping it off with his sword against a log while the soldier held his own wrist artery. Then Brian went to attend to another wounded man, took off his brassard for the blue jacket who was going to carry him back—and was killed. The soldier was carried on board, weak from loss of blood, but as he lay back on the stretcher, he was twirling his moustache with his one hand and smiling a faint, disdainful smile—looking neither to right nor left—"We got to be great friends with *him*."

Next day Dorothea set off to visit friends in Victoria. Her first destination was The Convent of the Sacred Heart, home of Mère Robin, one of the two "sweet Ladies of Grace" she had met three years earlier on her way to England.

SYDNEY — TRAIN

Extraordinarily tired. I suppose it was partly the going away and partly the conversation with Doctor Faithfull, who is very miserable (though brave) about his son's going to the War, but I did feel the heavy and the weary weight of all the unintelligible world—more than usual. Father looked worried, and Mother tired, and **I loved them much more than usual and was conscious it wasn't nearly enough!** Father came to see me off at the station. The night was stiflingly hot and one couldn't sleep, but the orange-coloured sickle of the moon, with the trees continually dodging in front of it, was good to see.

Monday
January 18

TRAIN — SACRED HEART

Tuesday January 19

It got hotter and hotter, and I never saw the drought worse than it is on the border. Made an inadequate rhyme on the red-and-silver of it, and read the magazines that a kind lady lent me, and was glad I don't look hot when I am. Then a scorching hot wind rose, and our unfortunate engine driver must have been half blinded—or quite blind—from the clouds of white dust. The train had to go slowly and we reached Melbourne an hour late. Mr Lyons of the Bank, and the bank messenger, were there to meet me (cursing me, I don't doubt) and the former insisted on taking me off to lunch. I believe, from his manner, that he was afraid I was going to faint. If the journey had lasted fifteen minutes longer I think I should have done so. And dirt has a very depressing effect.

The Chablis bucked me up, and I continued my travels through a really terrific dust-storm—cool this time, and the convent seemed at the world's end. But at last we saw its red walls rising out of a great garden. Mère Robin ran to meet me with her black veils fluttering about her sandalled feet, and kissed me very sweetly. Then I met the Reverend Mother . . . and she sent me to bed immediately. I had a beautiful bath—oh! the joy of it!—and slept like a child . . .

Her brief sojourn at the convent was followed by visits to several friends, including Lorna Smith at Duncraggan near Mt Macedon. In mid-February she returned to Sydney.

Thursday March 25

. . . Met Ruth at Circular Quay at 7 minutes to 10, and went over the sparkling water to Athol, where we sat on a de'little beach and looked at Sydney, pale and clear and beautiful. Then we watched a man casting a net, but he didn't finish. So we went into the bush and sat on a big grey rock and did Savill's Dream, and then to a maidenhair bank and did the real Savill, and then along the beginning of that twisting path (resisting the lure of the Taronga Zoo). And we sat under a tree dangling our feet over the Harbour, and lo an' bold [*sic*] another net was being drawn almost below us. So we ran and looked at the jumping silver fish, and by and by we went on and met the breeze round the corner, and played in a mysterious massive old stone place quite near a father and mother and baby, and on again—oh the path was lovely! It wound and climbed through beautiful bush, but never quite lost sight of the sea, and the water changed from ruffled turquoise to clear pale green, and deep red, and purple and dark green, and pale transparent blue and back to turquoise again, and at one moment big ships were passing by and at the next you'd think it was an undiscovered mountain tarn, so quiet and lovely it was.

And all the time we played, right over to Clifton. The water was splendid—one hardly had to swim at all, but it was quite rough. Then we came out and sunned ourselves and caught the boat back (I unwilling) and that beautiful day was over—the sun an enormous red ball that sunk into pearl-grey shadow—

... Mr Angas came in the evening and we all had a good talk—a grumble, I'm afraid, but there's a shocking lot to grumble about. And—once in a way—it does good. News of . . . Dudley North commanding 150 armoured Rolls Royces in Belgium, and flying and seeing life. And Death—

Sunday March 28

... In the afternoon we went to the Bank to watch the route march of the troops. They looked very well indeed. In the place of honour came the French reservists from Noumea, very workmanlike in their blue, with berets that had a red tassel on top. Then the Light Horse, a fine lot of men, so brown and lithe—and all the rest. They marched beautifully, and the long brown caterpillar with blue-white glitter of steel over it seemed endless. It gave one to think—

The crowd were quiet, which is better than yelling. The time to shout hasn't come yet . . .

Saturday April 24

The next part of the diary is lost. It resumes on July 7 with Dorothea "still feeling ill". The following evening Eric came to her in despair. Malcolm was planning to leave Kurrumbede. He had decided to accompany his friend, R. L. "Snowy" Baker, to Hollywood. Famous as an athlete and a boxer, "Snowy" Baker was also strikingly handsome. He was eager to try his hand as an actor, and hoped to persuade the American film-maker Claude Flemming to come to Australia and direct him in a film.

Malcolm's decision could not have come at a worse time. Not only was Kurrumbede seriously affected by drought, but Australia was at war and few men were left to work the properties. With Malcolm away, the responsibility of running Kurrumbede would fall on Eric. And there was more: on his return from America, Malcolm intended to enlist as a soldier and marry Enid Wolfe, a beautiful girl from Perth.

... **as I was going to bed Eric came in and I thought he wanted to talk—so he did and broke down worse than I have ever seen him!** Talked for 2½ hours, so there was time to say a good deal. **Malcolm had hurt badly—I am angry about it**—And there were other things. **Mac and a woman, for instance! And marriage**—Didn't sleep much.

Thursday July 8

Friday
July 9

Went to Dr Thring— . . . He was exceedingly nice to me. Nothing has gone wrong, I'm glad to say. Just general debility—sort of suppressed nervous breakdown! . . .

On July 20 she goes to Kurrumbede. Though some entries are lost, those remaining tell of a long and happy visit, with plenty of gardening. Malcolm has not yet left for America, and Eric is again in good spirits. From time to time Dorothea records the war news. On September 10 she visits country friends for a few days, and is back in Sydney by September 24.

Sunday
September 26

Stolen morning at Chester [Ruth's house]. Very good—Only a little of Mrs Conway and Innes-Howe, but it's a relief. In the afternoon the Parents dropped me at Manning Road, but I found that Mr Milne had died the day before, and Mrs Milne was very ill from shock. Poor things! And yet—

In the evening I packed books and wrote very many letters. Dad is worried to death with these census and income cards, and no one can help him.

In October the Mackellar family returned to Dunara in Wolseley Road, Rose Bay.

Friday
October 8

. . . We got straight very quickly, but our feet felt as if they were dropping off, and the first two nights they hurt me so that I couldn't sleep. It was fun arranging the different rooms, and Mother has given me a beautiful Persian rug about which I still feel guilty, and yet it makes me happy whenever I look at it—it is so satisfying. The movers and packers were rather nice, though their waggons ploughed the lawn. "It's rainin'—and I'm perspirin'." Two perfectly obvious facts. Such a long procession staggering past me in the cold, gravel-grimed draughty hall! Such strength—and bewilderment, and interest—and weariness. And shame at losing oneself in trivial private affairs while the world is being torn in two—

Although the diary entries are lost, Dorothea was soon once again at Kurrumbede, where she wrote several poems, including "On Kelly's Ridge".

OPPOSITE: *The Edge of the Forest* Frederick McCubbin

On Kelly's Ridge

As I was walking along my lone
  between the dusk and the light,
On Kelly's Ridge where the cattle graze,
  I saw a curious sight.
For sitting at ease on a resting cow
  and watching me cool and kind,
As if he'd been there for a hundred years,
  was the queerest man you'd find.

With the queerest wild thing's face on him,
  and the queerest furry clo'es
As it might be Puck . . . or a Leprechaun . . .
  or the great god Pan—who knows?
And "Why are you so low in your mind
  this fine cool night?" said he.
"No trouble's the sweeter for bottlin' up,
  so you'd better tell it to me."

He'd a quick curved mouth and a quick brown face
  and a wonderful quick brown hand
That was magicking over the cow's soft ears
  and I knew he'd understand—
For O his eyes were quiet and clear!—
  if I told him all my fret,
But how in the mischief he knew of it
  I hadn't wondered yet.

It's easier speaking of hidden things when
  the dusk is drawing in
And for all his smile he'd a master's look,
  so I didn't wait to begin:
I said, "I'm thinking my youth goes by . . .
  and I've not the lives of a cat,
And there's a weakness in all my bones—
  I'm thinking I'm young for that.

I feel I'm a drag on the rest of them
  . . . I know I'm getting worse,
For I haven't the strength to work at all,
  and that is a heavy curse,
And there's whiles I think that I've wasted
  my life and made my choice like a fool—"
And so I talked on, and he never spoke,
  but watched me kind and cool.

He and the cow seemed contented-like,
  and I told him what I think.
The while the sky at the back of them turned
  Yellow and green and pink.
He seemed a bit of the earth himself,
  and when I was fairly through,
"You think too much of yourself," he said,
  "and that's the matter with you."

Well now, if I wasn't angry then! I'd made up
  my mind you see
That he'd be saying some sort of charm
  that would magic the grief from me.
The night had come on us all at once,
  and I stood there dumb as a stone
While the heifer scrambled up to her feet
  and she and I stood alone.

I'd nothing to do but stump home again,
  through the dark and the owls that cried,
His chuckle echoing in my ears, and
  hurt in my decent pride
That I should have talked to a stranger so
  —but in spite of all I can do
It goes through me like a small cold wind
  that perhaps what he said was true.

Again a break, then:

174

[SYDNEY] . . . Everything was thickly veiled in creamy bushfire smoke (the whole of the Blue Mountains are burning) and all day the sun had been a flaming scarlet ball. Flame-colour and rose on Double Bay. Sat on the lawn in the cool dark.

Sunday
November 14

Cooler and heaps of hot and cold winds and a dust storm. There were odd feelings in the air—Mother didn't feel well, and Ruth came in the morning and I felt constrained to keep her all day, but we were quietly sleepy and sick . . . Tuesday was a glorious day to feel and see, and I got through a good deal too. But *what* does it matter—oh *what* does it matter?

Monday-Tuesday
November 15–16

A few days later Malcolm sailed for America with "Snowy" Baker, and Dorothea went to Kurrumbede, where Eric was having problems.

[KURRUMBEDE] The wheat is being handled disgracefully—wheat humpers at £2 a day, half of them lazing nags, with 26 teams waiting to unload—and 80,000 sacks stacked *outside*, while the shed (for which Mackellar Bros. have paid, and will hold at least 100,000) is empty— . . .

Friday
November 26

War news not good, but apparently K. of K. [Kitchener of Khartoum] is securing the neutrality of Greece.

Hot clear weather and starlit nights. No sign of rain . . . Janet T. Hoots the Bonegatherer (with a piece of mosquito-net over her face) will have a rich harvest* . . .

Sunday-Tuesday
November 28–30

. . . It felt stormy and strange. Blood-like, some few drops of rain.

Monday-Tuesday
December 6-7

DUNARA

There was a cool change on Tuesday night and consequently one arrived sick and shivering, but it was nice to be home . . . Saturday was a beautiful summer day, warm and cool blue and gold—green with the coral trees flaming everywhere so splendidly that it was like a thousand trumpets. As I walked down Wolseley Road I had a strange swinging feeling—and then suddenly I realized what it

Wednesday-Saturday
December 8-11

harvest: Because stock were not hand-fed during periods of drought, many animals died. The bones were collected by itinerant workers and sold to fertiliser factories.

175

was—that if there were no War (what an If!) I'd be happy. Not for years have I had that.

The record of the next ten months has gone, apart from fragments which indicate that Sir Charles developed pleurisy in February 1916, and that when he recovered Dorothea holidayed with Ruth in the Blue Mountains. In July she visited Kurrumbede. Malcolm was home from Hollywood. With him were "Snowy" Baker and Claude Flemming, who had agreed to direct "Snowy" Baker in a film, much of which would be shot at Kurrumbede.

In August Britain urgently requested Australia to provide additional soldiers. Although Prime Minister Hughes was empowered to introduce conscription, he had no choice but to consult the people, by means of a referendum. The issue released passionate sentiments. "You will not heed the foolish cry that you are sending men to their death," beseeched the pro-conscriptionists. "Only four are killed out of every hundred, so you are sending ninety-six to glory and victory." Amid anti-conscriptionist fears that Hughes was seeking to destroy the freedom of the working class, a one-day strike was called in protest.

Tuesday
October 3 1916

[SYDNEY] . . . Wondered if the Stop-Work Meeting on the morrow would mean much rioting. The IWW* intend to agitate for a general strike.

Wednesday
October 4

The wettest day I have ever known. It effectually damped the Stop-Work Meeting. About 60 men turned up, *and no leaders*, which was rather mean . . .

Friday
October 6

I went to Hughes' meeting for women at the Town Hall. It was a wonderful thing. I got there at 2.20 (meeting to begin at three) placing my trust in my platform ticket, but the place was crammed, passages and all, from gallery to basement, and thousands were turned away. Did get in, somehow, and most were very kindly, and finally hoisted me out of the crush onto the edge of the packed platform, whence I heard fairly well and had a good view of all the interruptions—Adela Pankhurst semaphoring in the Eastern gallery, and later a *blessé légère* . . . shouting "Traitor! Traitor!" to the Labour Socialist Mrs Dillon,

IWW: Industrial Workers of the World (the "Wobblies"), a radical workers' association founded in Chicago in 1905.

OPPOSITE: *Sydney Harbour by Night* Jane Price

who was speaking in favour of compulsion. On the whole it was a wonderfully orderly meeting, considering what a high pitch everybody was at, and I was proud of my sex when there was a loud and smoky explosion in the Eastern gallery—something apparently went wrong with the flashlight photography—and nobody turned a hair except one male assistant, who fainted . . . Hughes spoke very well, and as for his speech, is it not written in the daily papers?

Came out quite limp in spite of all my unknown and kindly protectresses . . .

The Sydney Morning Herald *carried the full text of Prime Minister Hughes' fiery pro-conscription speech. He said, ". . . You must ask yourselves the question 'What will my vote do? Shall I by my vote plunge a dagger into the heart of my country? Shall I abandon my children at the Front, my brother or my husband?' 'Never!' " came the cry from the floor.*

When the interjector mentioned by Dorothea could not be silenced, Hughes signalled to the organist, who struck up "Rule Britannia". The Sydney Morning Herald *observed, "That men interjected on occasion at public meetings was a well-known fact, but that there should be interjections at a meeting of women which the Prime Minister was addressing was an unheard-of thing." At the end of the meeting almost every woman raised a handkerchief, a glove or an umbrella in support of conscription.*

<table>
<tr><td>*Tuesday*
October 10</td><td>Grey oppressive day in which there was some time over, and I felt I could begin nothing—and suddenly I began to scribble the S's D [Savill's Dream] thing, after all these months . . .</td></tr>
<tr><td>*Friday*
October 20</td><td>In the morning, feeling very tired and feeble and cross, I wrote an article*</td></tr>
</table>

article: Entitled "Faint Heart and Tender Heart", it said in part: "It is no use to talk to the shirkers, men or women, nothing will change them. But they are, thank Heaven, in a minority. There are many others who mean to do their duty, but as yet do not see it clearly—or rather, the one clear thing in their minds is that conscription is a word they have always disliked. None of us like it; we do not like going to the dentist either, but it is very necessary for most of us now and then, if we are to remain useful and healthy members of society . . . The anti-conscriptionists have tried to trouble us with that cowardly question: 'Would you vote to send away another woman's son?' It sounds terrible; but, however tender-hearted we are, we hardly have the right to shrink from that. There is no hour of our lives when we are not dependent, unconsciously perhaps, and certainly without protest, on the suffering, the danger, the deaths of other women's sons—and daughters . . ." (*Sydney Morning Herald,* 25 October 1916)

for next week's *Herald*, as the Referendum Committee had requested, and in the afternoon went into town with Mother.

. . . Mrs Foster came to tea. She asked me to go to England with her. Why not to the moon?

Thursday October 26

Sir Ronald Munro Ferguson [Governor-General] invested Dad with the insignia of the Order of St Michael and St George. Incongruous and touching ceremony— **Dear Dad!** Met his friend Sir Thomas Ewing.* Quickbrained—sparring for an impression, too! . . .

Friday October 27

October 28 was Referendum Day. In spite of Dorothea's pro-conscription rhetoric, she was not surprised when she learnt that the majority of Australians were against conscription.

Sunday   October 29
As we feared, there's an overwhelming No within NSW, Q. and SA. But the other States aren't disgraced . . . I can't bear to talk about the Referendum, and everyone wants to.

Tuesday   November 14
A violent headache coloured the day for me—indigo blue and glaring streaks of light . . . Mother has been buying kerosene, etc., for we all expect to be in darkness unless the coal strike is settled within the next few days.

The last entry for 1916 is dated November 15. The record for January and March 1917 is lost, and only a few pages survive for February.

Wednesday   February 28 1917
. . . A letter from Eric—the IWW have burned down the hayshed, causing tremendous loss.

  I hope they'll catch the brutes—Oh poor Eric— it makes one furious.

Sir Thomas Ewing: For 35 years a politician, first in the Legislative Assembly and then in the Federal Parliament. Minister for Home Affairs 1906–07 and for Defence 1907–08, he was renowned for his ability and quick-wittedness.

A new journal begins on April 24 with Dorothea planning a visit at Kurrumbede.

Saturday–Monday
May 19–21
[KURRUMBEDE] On Saturday Dolly [the maid] went away in a thick 'but entertaining cloud of lies, which means a little more housework. But not much! . . . Glorious weather, but as dry as Dives' throat. Major, the very best draught horse picked up poison and died in agony. **Eric is so wonderful about that sort of thing!**

Monday
May 28
Now Lady Jane has died and Lord Jim is very ill.

Sunday–Monday
June 3–4
Nice days of yarns and gardening. I planted all the grape and passion vines on Sunday (and the rabbits ringbarked them that night). On Monday Eric and I drove over the wheat to see where the cattle had broken through. Lots of brolgas were stalking about, devouring. One had to be shot as a Warning. Such a magnificent grey and scarlet creature, with jade green beak—it was horrible to see it struck out of life, though one didn't wish to sentimentalize—

GUNNEDAH — SYDNEY

Tuesday–Wednesday
June 5–6
On Tuesday Douglas and I wired-in the vines, and on Wednesday I packed, which always takes so much longer than one expects, if done thoroughly—and went away . . . **I love Eric so hard it hurts all the time**, but it's warm too . . .

Tuesday–Wednesday
June 19–20
Tuesday was certainly the coldest morning I've ever known in Sydney. I wore my fur coat in the attic all the morning and wasn't really warm . . .

Nice sleepy evening with the Parents. Finished typing 2nd part of Savill's Dream. On Wednesday we began a clearing up at the BBC—all the old Municipal Library books to be sorted and dusted. Filthy work and tiring, but interesting too. We didn't get finished . . . To bed early, and waked by a gorgeous and irresistible gale at 1.30. Lasted with increasing violence till morning and is still going on (8 a.m.).

... About 6 o'clock Dad came home and opened his letter from Mac, who has been recommended for a commission in the 1st Life Guards by Lord Penrhyn, the OC who made special application to the War Office to have Mac's papers back, so that he shouldn't have to go through the regulation training. We're very proud **but my heart sank when Mother told me—the training much shorter, and the danger greater**— ...

I went to Randwick Hospital . . . and then to tea with Beulah.* The tram guard wanted "a lend o' my duck" i.e. pelican muff . . .

My birthday and a nice day too. Everybody was very sweet to me, especially the Parents, and I felt absurdly young part of the time. Played with Dad, and Ruth came after lunch. We talked most of the afternoon of the Winchcombes and of "plunging" [gambling], which Ruth says she congenitally can't! . . .

Malcolm, c. 1917

To-day was unlike any other, for I did everything that I had to do. (But the most important things I didn't do well!) Called to see Mrs Norman Pilcher and her new girl—baby—a darling—and did other calls, and letters and a rhyme or two.

. . . Lilian came . . . Nice days in spite of the west wind. There was sun too, and we knitted and yarned and played restfully. Lilian taught me how to knit two socks at once. The mechanics of it is easy, but it needs a deal of attention at first! . . .

. . . Mother and I went to see the war pictures (*Battle of the Ancre*) at the Town Hall. They were good and I was glad to see them, but somehow I was unspeakably tired afterwards—of course it was very long. The white strained faces of the wounded—

Beulah: Beulah Bolton, secretary of the Bush Book Club.

Ruth's birthday . . .

AUGUST 2 1917

Would to God, my Dear, my Dear
* That to you this hour*
Peace and Heartsease I could bring.
Nay, but Death is on the wing;
Man is grass that, withering,
* Shows a scarlet flower.*

Birthday wishes to my Ruth
* In an evil hour*
When the air is full of death
And Desire's self perisheth,
Only Love endures, and Truth —
* Only they have power.*

. . . The tramway engineers "came out", which probably is going to be serious. The trams are still going—just dribbling. On Friday I was to have left for Ben Buckley. I felt very unwell, and it was a beastly day, and finally the Parents were so worried about the long night journey etc. that Dad really was in earnest— and I should have been a brute to go. He was afraid of the strike cutting off communications, of course, and I was really rather afraid myself, on *his* account. So I telegraphed to Lorna and remained.

The third anniversary of the declaration of war—

Wednesday was spent in town—silent because of the tram strike—and with Mabel Nicholas and her two babies . . . Mabel asked me to be god-mother with Ruth—but really we all seem to be absurdly unorthodox—

A piercingly beautiful Spring day full of strikes and wars and pathos and irritation— and one felt as if one had several skins too few . . .

. . . Walked out to Rose Bay by the harbour's edge. What a hilly, cliffy place Sydney is—steep steps and sudden turns, with silken blue water at the end of every lane and oleander and pomegranate over the garden wall—

. . . The strike spreads and spreads, though the trams and railwaymen are dribbling back. The bakers haven't come out yet.

The pittosporum in full bloom and a south east wind . . .

On Monday Dorothy Macmillan, bless her clean, human heart, came and "spent the day", just as we had planned, and on Tuesday morning Ruth came and we had a little acting and a violent fit (at least I had) of restless blues. Reds and purples, rather . . . Dreadfully tired and restless and sick of being in one place. The tram strike's officially over, but by no means done with.

Went to Ruth and arranged rocklilies in a copper bowl. **Restless always.** Spring? And other things.

I got a War Chest hat in town, and did many other things, finishing up with the cyclamen and orchids in the Gardens—a glory of purple and rose and purest white. They're wonderful this year. So is the red and white peach blossom—
. . . Bee came in the afternoon, with her dog Paddy, who was very tired and fell into the fountain.

Woke very early with the joyful feeling of a holiday. It was a pretty, sunny day, though later on it turned cold, and I called for Ruth on my way back from Pyrmont (volunteer work . . .). We went out to Vaucluse [House]. It's much lovelier than I remembered. The wistaria is in full bloom, in curtains and garlands and great anaconda-coils all round the wide stone veranda, making little loopholes through which you watch the wreathed gay fountain and the clear forgetmenot sea; and the trees were glorious and the birds sang . . . and we thought of Pat [Patrick Chalmers] (who I hear today is probably married, bless him!) and thought how he'd love it all. We acted the Fosters and a very little of "Savill's Dream" for the sake of the staying.

On Tuesday night a terrific South-east gale began. It raged all Wednesday and did about £20,000 worth of damage in the eastern suburbs alone. I couldn't sleep for the howling of the wind and the pistol-shots of my canvas, but it was a nice cosy exhilarating contradictory night—when one didn't think of those at sea. Trees were torn down in all directions. It was the worst gale for very many years, and I wrote to Pat and did flowers (battered they were, and I was battered getting them) and Dorothy came in the afternoon. It *was* nice to have her.

Thursday
September 20

A perfectly glorious soft, cool, sun-warmed, sun-and-air-coloured day . . . and in the afternoon Mother and Dorothy and I went out to Vaucluse. The wistaria has been torn about, of course, and the roadway is stripped right down to its big rough bones and looks like the bed of a mountain torrent—but it's still beautiful . . . Dorothy . . . [and I] are just getting into our stride, and she'll have to go tomorrow, alas! At night we talked till the gas and electric light went out, and then talked on for ages in the dark!

Tuesday–Friday
September 25–28

Tuesday was pouring wet . . . and Lilian and I chased a Charlie Chaplin movie in the rain. We ran him to earth at last, but Rowe [the chauffeur] said it was hardly a place for her Ladyship . . . Friday was War Chest Day,* sunny and in fact hot. We bazaared in some excitement—Helen's black and orange stall very effective—and the Dods came in the afternoon. Violent headache.

Thursday
October 4

I went to the 19th Batt. Sale at the AJC rooms among a crowd of people to whom I used officially to belong, and whom I hadn't seen for years. Not bad, but I don't hunger to see them again. The things—vanities and children's clothes—were rather nice. Expensive of course, but then such things *are*, always.

Chester in the afternoon and a very tired Ruth. A hot, tropic day it was.

Tuesday
October 9

. . . The light restrictions were removed today.

Mac is to stay at Bisley* a month longer, to his disgust, with all the others. That looks well from every point of view.

On October 18 Dorothea left Dunara to visit Lorna Smith at Ben Buckley, near Mudgee. "Such miles of apple blossom—and lilac in masses, and pear and cherry bloom! . . . The Capertee Valley was clear blue and proudly silent."

Day: A massive fund-raising effort, for which hundreds of stalls were set up in the city. The day, which attracted huge crowds and began with a procession of decorated motor cars, raised £15,500 for the war effort.
Bisley: Army training centre in England.

Tuesday *October 23*	. . . I wandered away through lakes of bluebells . . . to the clear river, and meditated not quite fruitlessly, and paddled in cold clear water by the rapids till my feet were all pinky-white, and one small turquoise-headed dragonfly meditated at my side.
Monday *November 5*	[BEN BUCKLEY] . . .News—not confirmed that Russia has gone out of the war. "Armed Neutrality". Pray God it's not true.
Tuesday *November 6*	It's not, at least not yet . . . An offer from Angus & Robertson for the right to reproduce "My Country" with J. J. Hilder's illustrations.* This amuses me, but is nevertheless very welcome.
Tuesday *November 13*	. . . We're to have another Referendum about Conscription. It's hard to bear—because I don't see how it can *possibly* succeed—and one is so shamed.
Thursday *November 22*	[DUNARA] It rained hard. In the morning I made Ruth's calendar,* and went to Chester in the afternoon. Most of the war news is bad, but there's a great success on the Western Front, and Marconing taken.

Friday–Saturday December 14–22

[KURRUMBEDE] Went to Gunnedah on Friday night . . .[and] arrived 6 a.m. of a hot clear day. Drove out with Eric before breakfast, the garden a wilderness of sunflowers. Filled my apron with brand new ducklings like lightly poached eggs . . . On Monday Eric had to go and collect shearers in town—band shears—he's having a lot of bother . . . On Tuesday I wrote lots of notes and longed to write Deb* [a new novel], but on Wednesday I did a good deal of her . . . Thursday was Referendum Day,* and hot. We motored to Gunnedah

illustrations: In 1918 Angus & Robertson published *The Art of J. J. Hilder.* It included the poem "My Country", hand-lettered and illustrated by the artist.
calendar: From 1912 to 1932 Ruth Bedford and Dorothea Mackellar exchanged calendars each Christmas. Made from six sheets of beautiful heavy paper linked with ribbons, two months to a page, each calendar was painstakingly embellished with photographs, tiny reproductions of paintings, quotations, short poems, quatrains and couplets, carefully chosen to reflect a different theme for every page.
Deb: this novel was eventually given the title The Unbroken. It was not published.
Day: The majority of Australians were still against conscription.

by Gunnible. The river was too high to cross. It's a curious feeling to be so very much on the unpopular side (makes you cock your bonnet). Talked to Mattie Hargrave, whose son was killed at Gaza. He is glorious with pride. Says G'dah will be 3 to 1 *No* . . . On Saturday left Kurrumbede, pretty hot it was. I can't bear to write of the Referendum— . . .

Christmas Day

[DUNARA] A quiet veiled day. We all went to church, and were together a good deal. It was peaceful and very nice. Nobody came . . . and after tea it rained. The others read, and I wrote.

Saturday–Monday December 29–31

. . . I wrote most of the XVI Chapter and Dr Scot-Skirving, the dear, came in the evening. Dad talked eagerly, with a fire of youth in him. Bless them both— . . . Monday Wrote . . . Rain and Ruth, and a little acting at Chester. Parents in the evening, and then I wrote again and entirely forgot it was New Year's Eve.

. . . There's nothing in the papers but squabbles. Heaven knows what is really happening in the world.

Thursday
January 24 1918

. . . Bush Book Club and lunch with Beulah, aquatints at Horderns . . . I wanted three of them aquatints, including a green-and-silver moonlit sky—and it was a curious feeling that I *couldn't* buy them, because it would make me too uncomfortable. It was not unselfishness. But French children, and that soldier who's trying to start his job again—no, I couldn't. And yet I'm not helping.

Tuesday
February 5

. . . Beulah came in the morning to listen to Deb. I read it to her for 5 hours and got half through. She liked it.

Saturday
February 16

Did a lot of things in town, including the purchase of Kathleen's picture, and the dispatch of Deb to Eric . . . Hospital and clamorous children. I wasn't *nearly* enough to go round—and home, tearing off my heel, dog-tired. But not depressed, having fulfilled my day.

Tuesday
February 26

Friday *March 1*	In the morning I had a telegram from Miss Smith saying that cousin Lilian was very ill. In answer to my [telephoning] she said "condition unchanged" . . . so, in fact, it was better that I shouldn't come. Lilian died at eight o'clock that night.
Monday *March 11*	I went to town, saw R.L. (Snowy) in his "stunt" play—the stunts infinitely better than the yarn—and the Broun children came with Tot* in the afternoon.
Wednesday *March 13*	. . . In the afternoon went to see Mr Dods and Dorothea Mayo, and talked about Families. "All that affection is dulling," she said. Lord, where does she find it? If there were more affection there'd be less dullness— . . .
Tuesday *March 26*	. . . The great battle still going on. News not over-cheerful, and one can't think of anything else. And one *daren't* dwell on all that it means.
Wednesday *March 27*	. . . Wrote heaps of notes, mainly condolences. The news no better.
Sunday *March 31*	[EASTER SUNDAY] Church, and a long yarn to Eric. I might get mixed up in this new Australian "movie"*—Fun!
Thursday *April 18*	The news from France is still as serious as it can be. Bad, but fluctuating—We have lost in 2 weeks what took 2 years to gain.

Monday April 22

. . . Jean Curlewis [Ethel Turner's daughter] came in the afternoon—a rosy Peggy-like young thing with beautiful grey-green eyes. Adoration, very strong but simple—I must say it's a pleasant drink.

Tot: "Tot" Broun, Dorothea's friend, wife of Reg Broun, owner of Colstoun, a property near Kurrumbede.
"movie": the silent film *Lure of the Bush* with "Snowy" Baker, directed by Claude Flemming. Eric played a bushranger, and "Tot" Broun was the nurse.

OPPOSITE: *Still Life* Roy de Maistre

Friday morning I spent in town with Dad, calling on his little friends (Dr Mary Booth at the Soldiers Club and Dr Armit at the BMA). Great pride I had seeing the British Army badges on the wall, with the 1st Life Guards' heading them, the same that I wore on my breast— . . . On Saturday (very tired) . . . to Ruth. She had a cold. We didn't act much, but talked—Suppressed anxiety I think.

But on Saturday morning came a cable dated May 2 from France to say that Mac was well there.

Dad and I drove down to Hunter's Hill to the Armits. Clever restless thing he is, with (I *think*) a German wife—poor dear, beef to the heels but musicianly . . .

Got through a lot of letters while the sirens hooted and a camouflaged troopship drew slowly past the mouth of Rose Bay to the Heads. Blue-red, gold-green, the day, and the ship violent black and white.

Eric, Ruth and I set out in the R.R. for Kurrajong—a beautiful hot day—and got up after being delayed by a blow-out at Gladesville, a tuck-in at Windsor, and Rowe's cold-footedness at the last hill. E. returned, and R. and I walked a little and played. Mainly Chesters. On Friday there was a beastly west wind. We sheltered down the gully with the friendly small birds (firetails, fantails, wrens, robins, etc.) in a wattle-grove, and then among the ferns, and did Briar and Jock. (Blue Lagoonish.) One couldn't walk with much pleasure, or sit down except under shelter. It was awfully cold, but clear as crystal . . .

On Sunday we walked down the Cut Rock Road—a most beautiful fairy-malory-robin-hooded place, and 2 miles from Avilion, maybe, or Babylon or Elfland, and played the Chesters in deep bracken at Merrow and Jock Lamont on a walking tour. We rested in the afternoon, and next day, the first still one— lay in the sun on the lawn and did the Geoffrey Wares, and a scissors-grinder [a bird] talked to us from a tree. On Tuesday, the weather continuing to be beautiful, we went down the hill, not as far as the gully, and acted Mr Savill in a slightly repentent mood. Such a relief after all those months. At night too—and the dear Chesters, very young and happy at present. On Wednesday we walked in the opposite direction. Diarmid's Look Out—glorious. Did the Babes in the Wood and various others—Claire I think. It's such a pity we don't feel inclined for Pippa, in these surroundings. On Thursday we walked far along that same road and did Tony and Glynde letting off steam so that the fire shouldn't get too hot—most satisfactory. Home just in time for lunch, and we took our tea out, and played Briar and Jock, and the Rylands, and Deb and Bill to a fat bold yellow robin, Chesters, Lawlesses (Savill had been a brute to Jenny) and Geoffrey Ware in the evening. On Friday we packed and played Briar and Jock with Harry's flight etc., and left. A lovely drive with a crabby but amusing driver . . . Home and dear Family—

Town, with an unexpected broken-kneed cab-horse instead of a taxi. Chores and BBC. Eleven o'clock from Miss Helen Bolton, who implores me again to write a Poem on a Sunset, and offers raw cake as a reward . . .

Wednesday
July 31

A.I.F. Day.* Went into town to the 20th Battalion Stall, after leaving R.'s birthday book. Then to greet her, then to give Miss Helen Bolton her piebald poem, and afterwards to lunch with Eric. Then he and I went to see the private run(?) of *The Call of the Bush.** Some of it is excellent, but Barrett's* genteel titles are awful . . .

Friday
August 2

. . . A mail (the first for a month) came in, with many letters from Mac. Good news . . . Eric went away. On Tuesday I was picking freesias and scarlet carnations in the windy garden when Mr R. L. Baker came, and we worked all the morning over titles for *The Call of the Bush*. In the afternoon Mother and I went to

Monday–Tuesday
August 5–6

Day: Australian Imperial Forces Day, another fund-raising effort, during which 12,000 children marched through the city. The *Sydney Morning Herald* commented that such days were occurring every few weeks, during which one "would be set upon by an army of girl canvassers who know no mercy".
Bush: The title was changed to *Lure of the Bush* just prior to its release. The film was a great success. Posters advertised: "The station hands hopped up on the rails, while the worst brumby in the yards rooted and snorted and kicked to get rid of the jackeroo on his back. But that jackeroo rode him to a standstill. Just see him do it!"
Barrett's: Walter Franklyn Barrett, cameraman for *Lure of the Bush*.

ABOVE: A scene from the movie

John Reid and talked Earlston* alterations for a long time . . . Worked ("titles") at night.

| Thursday August 8 | "Snowy" Baker's rooms, with titles to the accompaniment of the punching ball. Barrett is hard to manage; the poor thing has no idea how people speak—he's horribly polite: "That tahd" etc... |

Thursday August 8

"Snowy" Baker's rooms, with titles to the accompaniment of the punching ball. Barrett is hard to manage; the poor thing has no idea how people speak—he's horribly polite: "That tahd" etc...

Saturday August 10

Felt very ill—the humiliation of "nerves"— . . . Finished typing "Titles" at night.

Wednesday August 14

I went into town. Stevenson, the new chauffeur, drives well and in other matters is pathetically anxious to do his best, but Sol Green* wasn't *really* a good preparation for driving our so-private, modest car . . .

Friday August 16

. . . After lunch I went in the car and the rain to Govt. House, the 19th Batt. and Smith and Julius' office. S. Ure Smith* is nice—simple and quiet. Bertram Stevens was there too. We talked shop and curiously enough I *didn't* feel shy of it—and after he went, Leon Gellert* came in—a nice young thing with a fine fair face. It looks as if it were eternally facing a wind with its chin up. Not strong, and his returned soldiers' badge significant on his shoulder. I didn't have time to see half the pictures, but I saw the Hilder book as far as it has got . . .

Monday August 26

A well-filled day of Jack's Day* meetings, BBC and "trade runs" of the film. Eric introduced me to the darlingest little black cocker spaniel puppy, six weeks old today . . . His birthday present to me. In the evening I wrote two articles for Jack's Day, and at night the new baby wept till I took her to bed with me. Bless her.

Wednesday August 28

Spent the morning doing flowers (carrying the exigent Sheila about in the pocket of my apron, like a mother-wallaby) . . .

Earlston: a large house on 12 acres of land at Warrawee, purchased by Lady Mackellar on August 2.
Green: Before joining the Mackellars, Stevenson had worked for Solomon Green, a flamboyant and philanthropic businessman renowned for his gold-plated Rolls Royce.
Ure Smith: Sydney Ure Smith, with Bertram Stevens and Charles Lloyd-Jones, co-editor of the magazine *Art in Australia*, published first by Angus & Robertson and later by Sydney Ure Smith.
Leon Gellert: Co-editor of *Art in Australia* after the death of Bertram Stevens.
Day: A fund-raising for Australian sailors.

Thursday
September 5

Bitterly cold and I probably have a chill. Anyhow the depression is acute, with very little to account for it, as the news is still good. And I missed Sheila at night. She has been removed to the wood-house.

THE YOUTHFUL SHEILA

Awhile upon my feet she lies
In vacant or in pensive mood
Ere barking to the gate she flies
To slay the wretch who dares intrude;
And then her heart with pleasure fills,
She dances on the daffodils.

Tuesday
September 10

A very beautiful day for the French Mission to enter the harbour. I washed Sheila and wrote some letters, feeling exhausted thereby. I'm *sick* of feeling ill! But—the news is good.

Wednesday
September 11

Played my new game of six-months-to-live with some success . . . In the evening Father and I went to a big affair at Government House for the French Mission. Nervous and disinclined, as is usual these days—but General Pau is a *dear.* And it really was nice to see one's friends, even in that crowd . . .

Monday
September 16

. . . Stood till my innards felt like dropping out to look at the Hackett Sale (nice jade and ivory) and would have dissipated at a Movie, had there been one worth seeing. But I didn't feel I could bear any I saw from the outside. A queer day—it's ages since I felt as if I had so much time, and yet I *should* have been doing things. Very wrong. And tiring.

Wednesday–Friday
September 18–20

Washed Sheila and read for BBC till the afternoon, when Mother and I went to tea with Mrs Simpson. Letters in the evening. These days aren't bad, really, though they sound pretty hopeless. The news not much, but not bad either. On Thursday I went to Chester and played Alison with the frivolous Ruth . . . Friday was extremely hot and I felt inclined to follow the example of the young lady of Tottenham* . . . Half-hearted attempt at summer shopping . . .

Went to the opening of the Society of Artists' Exhibition. There were some nice things by Norman Lindsay, Elioth Gruner and Howard Ashton, and I like Leason's even better than before . . . but the things one would have wished to buy were all "sold", "not for sale" or "kindly lent". I did get a L. Lindsay though, *faute de mieux.*

TO NORMAN LINDSAY ON AN OLD GRIEVANCE

The Grecian nymphs we read about
Were slim and shy and fleet,
And quite a lot depended on
The swiftness of their feet.
So Lindsay of the Master-Hand
I take it rather hard
That you should make them solid vrouws *
Who could not run a yard.

They couldn't run as you depict,
Their wind is lost in fat.
The slowest satyr'd give it up,
There'd be no fun in that.
Either, in racing through the hills
As naked as the moon,
The heavy hips and flopping breasts
Would sweat to slimness soon
Or else they'd quit the woodland sports
Like wallflowers self-effacing—

A nymph who cannot run for nuts
Is hardly worth the chasing.

. . . Got news that the Boche has accepted Wilson's peace terms. Now we'll wait and see.

Tottenham:
   "There was a young lady of Tottenham
   Whose manners, Good Lord! she'd forgotten 'em.
   When she went to the vicar's,
   She took off her knickers,
   Because she said she was hot in 'em."

vrouws: Matrons (Dutch).

<table>
<tr><td>Wednesday
October 16</td><td>. . . At night [went] to see C. E. Monteith in hospital. A nice, goodlooking boy. He showed me the bit of bone they got from his leg, which was not his. He was rather nice about it—natural and not callous . . .</td></tr>
<tr><td>Thursday
October 17</td><td>Hot wind—the first . . . Peace rumours, which one can't believe—burst.</td></tr>
<tr><td>Saturday–Sunday
October 19–20</td><td>. . . There was a creamy full moon in a windy green sky. And the news is good—they've evacuated the Belgian coast.</td></tr>
<tr><td>Thursday
October 24</td><td>Ruth came and we were both too tired to act. We think it's the good news too—we haven't the same frantic need to escape from ourselves.</td></tr>
<tr><td>Sunday–Wednesday
November 3–6</td><td>[KURRUMBEDE] . . . Drought—drought. Teal and black duck at the lagoon, and lots of plover. On Monday I had a spurt of energy and used some of it to make a List of Projects—in the old childish way. But it did carry me on a bit too. Tuesday and Wednesday I spent in bed, except for the evenings. Eric was away in the daytime. On Wednesday night he played the gramophone,</td></tr>
</table>

 which made me want to cry—"the laugh that brings the groan—"

All this time the news is good. On Wednesday Austria surrendered unconditionally.

Friday   November 8

A rumour came that the Armistice has been signed, but was almost immediately contradicted.

Saturday–Monday   November 9–11

. . . The news the papers brought was *good*. (I believe they went mad in Sydney yesterday.) . . . On Sunday the Brouns came, and in the evening Eric and I played penny-ante [mean-minded] billiards, a good game, and our minds were numb. On Monday at the end of a hot afternoon, a storm broke on us after waltzing completely round the horizon. I got soaked to the skin (which was pleasant) while rescuing the chicks and ducklings from flood.

I'll not forget the two tall dust-devils who strode across the plain just ahead of that black-purple storm. And in the evening Mr Reg Broun told us the Armistice had been signed.

The Armistice has begun. I can't take it in and don't feel excited. We drove in to Gunnedah just in time to hear—in the distance—the tail-end of the Royal Proclamation. The crowd was as might be expected, but they've closed all the pubs . . .

Tuesday
November 12

We couldn't sleep in the train . . . At practically every station on the way home they met the train with tootings and tin-cans. Very tired and restless, and useless all day. Ruth came in the afternoon. She's feeling much the same.

Wednesday
November 13

Felt decidedly ill . . . Rest, and *The New Book of Martyrs*, which at the present moment I find unbearable.

My dear family—"darlin's" all—

Friday
November 15

DOROTHEA MACKELLAR

POSTSCRIPT

Dorothea was 33 when the war ended. Malcolm returned to Australia, married Enid Wolfe, and settled at Kurrumbede with Eric. Dorothea and Ruth resumed their acting, though by the end of 1919 Dorothea was restless to see England again. Accompanied by Eric, she left Australia in February 1920. In England she stayed with her friend Meg McPhillamy, by then married to Hugh Scarlett (later Lord Abinger), renewed her acquaintance with Joseph Conrad, and visited Patrick Chalmers and his wife.

By February 1921 Dorothea had returned to her parents. A year later her third anthology of verse, *Dream Harbour*, was published. Sir Charles Mackellar was growing old, his memory began to fail, and he became increasingly infirm. In anticipation of retirement and uneasy at Earlston, which he found remote from the city and his old friends, he bought Rosemont, a beautiful Woollahra house later owned by the Lloyd-Jones family. A *Daily Telegraph* journalist who interviewed Dorothea at *Rosemont* wrote:

> . . . a wide vista of garden and lawn, flanked on one side by a tennis court and several summer houses. A rambling old house, with wide stone verandahs furnished invitingly with hammocks and lounges, served to intensify the first impression that here was quietness and peace.

Sir Charles retired in 1925, but little time remained for him, and on July 14 1926, aged 81, he died.

Dorothea felt her father's death keenly. She asked architect Hardy Wilson to build Tarrangaua, a quiet retreat for her at Lovett Bay, on Pittwater. Her fourth anthology, *Fancy Dress*, was published the same year. A new note of criticism began to be voiced. The English journal *Church Standard* wrote:

> In her appreciation of the beauty . . . of nature, we think that Miss Mackellar holds a really high place. When we turn from the nature poems . . . to those which touch on life, we feel a certain disappointment. We seem to be conscious of a note of uncertainty and an absence of real person. Chiefly we confess our disappointment springs from the conviction that Miss Mackellar is capable of something better than this . . .

In 1927 Dorothea consulted an astrologer:

> . . . marriage under *ideal* conditions awaits you, in Rangoon or Calcutta . . .Make
> for India as soon as you like. It's the right spot for you alright and holds all
> that life calls sweet in the realm of social success and romance . . . You live in
> the clouds at times, dreaming the hours away in a world of your making — . . . but
> later you will awake, and truly live, for a kindred soul will flash like a meteor
> across your horizon . . .

But a possible soul mate was left to languish in Rangoon. Instead Dorothea
and Lady Mackellar went to Europe for an extended visit.

Dorothea was in London when she learnt that Eric had married Anne Thornton
in October 1928. The marriage was sudden, and not without controversy, for
his bride was of lower social standing. Yet Dorothea was delighted at the news,
for she held herself partly responsible for the failure of the relationship between
Dorothy Owen and Eric 20 years earlier. Eric and Anne travelled to Europe
for their honeymoon. They planned to meet Lady Mackellar and Dorothea in
London, but on April 28 1929 the marriage came to an early and tragic end;
Anne died of a heart attack in Paris.

Following her return to Australia in 1930 Dorothea busied herself for a
while with the formation of Sydney branches of Zonta and the PEN (Publishers,
Editors and Novelists) Club. But by now Lady Mackellar's health was failing.
She suffered a stroke and died in 1933. Rosemont was sold and Dorothea bought
Cintra in Darling Point Road.

In 1933, too, Babs died. The MacGregors had retired to Scotland in 1914
and, following the death of her fiancé on active service, Babs went to live
in London. She never married. Her sister, Alpina Viti, wife of Commodore Sir
Alfred Paget, died in 1918. The next year both Sir William and Lady MacGregor
died, and Babs entered into a long and bitter legal battle with Viti's daughter
concerning Sir William's estate. Babs' health eventually failed, and she died
with the dispute unsettled.

Whilst Dorothea continued to write until 1943, possibly the last verse to
be published was "Psyche's Wings", printed in the *Sydney Morning Herald*
of April 6 1929. With a trend towards poetic modernism in the 1930s, interest
in her work (apart from "My Country", which enjoyed a special status) waned.

OPPOSITE: *The End of the Story* E. Phillips Fox

For some years she visited schools to listen as the children recited "My Country", but this activity ceased as she entered the second half of her life, away from public scrutiny.

After Anne's death, Eric succumbed to a depression, aggravated by alcohol, from which he never recovered. Kurrumbede was sold in 1939, and for the last ten years of his life Eric lived with Dorothea at Cintra. Dorothea, too, became increasingly dependent on alcohol and on the opiates for so many years the standard Australian prescription for pain and "nerves". She and Eric lived in growing seclusion, and her friends and acquaintances worried about her. "I do hope that 1939 will be happier and calmer for you," wrote Ethel [Turner] Curlewis:

> I imagined that you had come to quieter waters for the last year or two (and you were looking so well, it was easy to think so) but Ruth Bedford says no, you still have a choppy sea to contend with and the infinitude of caring for many others. Ah well, it's life, isn't it? There is no freedom, no peace anywhere—anywhere. Nothing to do but make believe we like it . . .

Meg (Lady Abinger) wrote from Inverlochy, Scotland, "I hope you will let us know how you really are. Can't you get well, Dorothea? Could a European doctor help you?"

Peace and health remained elusive, but one surprise remained. In 1941 she fell in love with a man younger than herself. For the first time in years she resorted to her almost forgotten code, practising the letters in the margin of her diary before recording his name. But the difference in their ages could not be ignored. Drily she wrote:

> *So we were made for each other?*
> *Bad staffwork then, that Fate*
> *Should fashion me so much too soon*
> *And you such years too late!*

The last poem listed in her versebooks, and dated 1942, is an epitaph for this brief-flowering love.

> *From the Sky*
> *Through the Flames*
> *To the Sea*
> *All Earth gone. Vale.*

Dorothea's overseas travels ceased with the death of her mother, though her friends and relatives in England and Scotland never tired of inviting her. Meg, in particular, was eager to see Dorothea again. She longed to come to Australia, but was incapacitated with arthritis; writing was often too much for her, travel was out of the question.

When Malcolm died in 1943, Dorothea was hospitalised. Her old friend Dorothy Macmillan (of the "clean, pure heart") recognised Dorothea's need for loving assistance and offered to live at Cintra "for a while". Dorothy outlived Dorothea by two years, and lived at Cintra for the rest of her life. Following Eric's death in 1950 Dorothea was frequently in hospital. When well enough, she returned to Cintra where she was cared for by Dorothy.

Dorothea's friendship with Ruth continued until Ruth's death in 1963. Ruth never married, but lived with her sister Freda. Two books of her poetry were published: *Sydney at Sunset* and (for children) *Rosycheeks and Goldenhead*. On a number of occasions Ruth attempted, unsuccessfully, to find a publisher for her children's stories. For several years she worked on a biography of the Stephens (her mother's family). Entitled *Think of Stephen*, it was well-received when published in 1955.

In 1967 Gordon Williamson, a great admirer of Dorothea's poetry, approached the New South Wales government with a request for formal recognition of her work. As a direct result of this, Dorothea was awarded an OBE for services to Australian literature in the 1968 New Year Honours. At that time she was in the Scottish Hospital, Paddington (originally The Terraces, where she had been a patient in 1911), receiving treatment for a broken hip. Whilst there, she suffered a stroke and, on January 14 1968, died in her sleep.

Isobel Marion Dorothea Mackellar OBE is buried in the family vault at Waverley Cemetery.

Acknowledgements

While every effort has been made to trace copyright holders,
the publishers tender their apologies for any unintended infringement.

Illustrations

Page viii   Hans Heysen 1877–1968 Australian
            A Summer's Day
            Watercolour
            73.6 x 54.0 cm
            Presented by John H. Connell
            (Collection of the National Gallery of Victoria)
Page 10   Dorothea, 1910 (Kath Strang)
Page 13   Mackellar family, c.1900, at Dunara (Kath
            Strang)
Page 14   Pages from Dorothea's diary (Mitchell Library)
Page 17   Dorothea, about sixteen (Mitchell Library)
Page 20   Lady Mackellar, c.1900 (Kath Strang)
Page 22   Keith Mackellar (Mitchell Library)
Page 23   Sir Charles Mackellar (Kath Strang)
Page 24   Dorothea's grandmother, Isobel Mackellar
            (Kath Strang)
Page 25   Dorothea's grandfather, Frederick Mackellar
            (Kath Strang)
Page 29   Mackellar family, c.1900, at Dunara (Kath Strang)
Page 31   Dorothea, c.1910 (Kath Strang)
Page 32   Illustration from *Art in Australia*, December 1921
Page 35   Illustration from *Ladies' Sphere*, December 1918
            (Mitchell Library)
Page 37   Rupert Bunny
            The garden bench c.1915
            oil on canvas 72.5 x 60
            Purchased 1923
            (Collection of the Art Gallery of
            New South Wales)
Page 38   Illustration from *Ladies' Sphere*, 1918
            (Mitchell Library)
Page 40   Roy de Maistre, Beach Scene, c.1917 (Goulburn
            City Collection, C. G. Moffitt Bequest)
Page 44   Illustration from *Australian Home Journal*,
            August 11, (Mitchell Library)
Page 48   Illustration from *Art in Australia*, December 1921
Page 51   Brisbane, c.1900 (From Australian Consolidated
            Press Library)
Page 53   Illustration from *Ladies' Sphere*, December 1918
            (Mitchell Library)
Page 55   Photo from Australian Consolidated
            Press Library
Page 56   Illustration from *Ladies' Sphere*, December 1918
            (Mitchell Library)

Page 57   Illustration from *Art in Australia*, no. 6, 1919
Page 60   Illustration from *Art in Australia*, no. 7, 1919
Page 62   Illustration from *Ladies' Sphere*, April, 1918
            (Mitchell Library)
Page 63   Illustration from *Ladies' Sphere*, April 1918
            (Mitchell Library)
Page 65   Roy de Maistre
            Australia 1894–1968
            Flowerpiece.
            oil on canvas
            55.5 x 46.5 cm
            (Collection: Australian National Gallery,
            Canberra).
Page 67   Illustration from *Ladies' Sphere*, December 1918
            (Mitchell Library)
Page 69   Illustration from *Art in Australia*, no. 9, 1921
Page 70   Illustration from *New Idea*, March 1911
            (Mitchell Library)
Page 72   "The Selection" (c.1915)
            Oil on canvas
            45.7 x 35.9 cm
            Inscribed: l.r. "JULIAN ASHTON"
            (Collection: Newcastle Region Art Gallery)
Page 76   Emanuel Phillips Fox 1865–1915 Australian
            Moonrise, Heidelberg, 1900
            Oil on canvas
            75.8 x 126.5 cm
            Purchased 1948
            (Collection of the National Gallery of Victoria)
Page 78   Illustration from *The Home*, February 1920
            (Mitchell Library)
Page 80   Illustration from *New Idea*, 6 April 1911
            (Mitchell Library)
Page 81   Thea Proctor
            The flowershop c.1919
            colour lithograph
            24.1 x 19.2 cm
            Purchased 1974
            (Collection of the Art Gallery of
            New South Wales)
Page 83   Illustration from *New Idea*, 6 April 1911
Page 85   Illustration from *Art in Australia*, no. 9, 1921
Page 86   Illustration from *The Home*, December 1920
            (Mitchell Library)